The Guide to Understanding the Insurance Industry

PUBLISHER **Arthur Snyder**
EXECUTIVE VICE PRESIDENT **Arthur Snyder III**
VICE PRESIDENT **Lee McDonald**
ASSISTANT VICE PRESIDENT **Marilyn Ostermiller**
EDITOR **Chris Sharkey**

ART & PRODUCTION
SENIOR MANAGER **Susan L. Browne**
DESIGNER **Judy Layman**
COVER ILLUSTRATION **Andrew Crespo**
ILLUSTRATION **Angel Negron, Debra DeVico**

Tell Us What You Think
Is this publication helpful to you? Did you find
the information you were looking for? What other
information do you wish we had included? Send your
thoughts to *news@ambest.com*

Library of Congress Control Number: 2007908099

Publisher: BookSurge Publishing
North Charleston, South Carolina

Visit *http://guides.ambest.com* to order additional copies.

An Insurance Primer

Things happen. No matter what steps you take to prevent unforeseen events, risk is a part of everyday life. Things happen.

While there's insurance to cover every aspect of your life or in the life of your business, ultimately, insurance is about being prepared for that day of days when the worst happens—a catastrophe hits.

In 2006, the Property/Casualty sector of the insurance industry caught a break—the hurricane forecast was a flop.

The industry's underwriting performance bounced back. Its 2006 profit of $31.2 billion was a sharp turnaround from the $7.3 billion year-end loss in 2005. A big reason was that only three tropical storms made landfall in the United States in 2006, a welcome respite from the previous two years, when nearly a dozen hurricanes caused tremendous losses.

It was also a busy year for health insurers, as the rollout of Medicare Part D and Medicare Advantage products led to a healthy 31.8% growth in revenues. In addition, the life insurance industry continued to benefit from strong equity markets and a gradual rise in interest rates, but a deep menu of factors—from increased mortality rates to real estate woes—could begin to eat away at its financial strength.

The insurance industry is a key player in the capital markets, with holdings in the trillions. But for an industry that manages risk and anticipates the what-ifs amid a fluctuating market and unprecedented challenges, its main purpose remains meeting the obligations of its policyholders, which is why A.M. Best's financial strength and debt ratings are so important.

This guide provides a large range of topics and tools necessary to understand how the industry earns and spends its money. Hopefully, it will shed some light on some questions you may have and provide information you didn't even know you needed.

And this is just the tip of the iceberg...

At **www.ambest.com**, you will find a wealth of information at your fingertips. Log onto **www.ambest.com** to find in-depth reports, multiplatform products pertaining to the insurance industry, up-to-the-minute insurance news and much more.

Athletes/Celebrities
Covered from Head to Toe

Can you pick out these famous figures from the crowd at right?

1 His "Lord of the Dance" legs are insured for nearly $40 million.

2 The St. Louis Cardinals took out a $12 million disability policy on this retired slugger.

3 This TV star is also the owner of the $10 million smile.

4 This legendary horse was insured for $10 million against failing a fertility test.

5 This New Jersey native had his voice covered for $6 million.

6 The $5 million face: Who is this supermodel?

7 This Rolling Stone took matters into his own hands by insuring his guitar fingers for $1.6 million.

8 This actress, singer and pin-up girl was known for her $1 million legs.

9 This two-time Academy Award-winning American actress had a $28,000 policy against weight gain.

10 Hollywood's silent comedian with the trademark walk had his feet insured for $150,000 in the 1920s.

11 In the 1940s, this crooner insured his prominent nose for $50,000.

See page 60 for answers.

Illustration by William Waggoner for A.M. Best Company

Table of Contents

WHAT DOES [IT] MEAN?
The bracketed number that follows the insurers' names is the A.M. Best-assigned number. In some cases, it may refer to a larger group. To learn more about these insurance companies and their Best's Ratings, visit **www.ambest.com/ratings**.

Agents & Brokers
Connecting with the Customer

WHO SELLS IT: Most insurance is sold through agents and brokers, but insurers also market their risk protection products directly through the mail, the telephone or the Internet.

GETTING PAID: Agents are paid commissions based on value and type of products they sell. Some insurers pay brokers additional compensation based on the performance of the business.

WHAT TO EXPECT: Questions that are usually asked with any insurance purchase are: Do I need it? How much do I need? Can I afford it?

At the Market: Brokers

Stock performance: A six-month look at the brokers indexes
(Six months ended 6/28/2007) Index, Dec. 31, 2004 = 1000

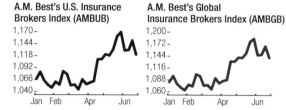

A.M. Best's U.S. Insurance Brokers Index (AMBUB)

A.M. Best's Global Insurance Brokers Index (AMBGB)

Top 10 Global Insurance Brokers

A look at the world's largest brokers with their 2005 and 2006 rankings.

Ranking 2006	Ranking 2005	Broker	Total Revenues 2006
1	1	Marsh & McLennan Cos.	$11.9 billion
2	2	Aon Corp.	9.0 billion
3	3	Willis Group Holdings Ltd.	2.4 billion
4	4	Arthur J. Gallagher & Co.	1.5 billion
5	5	Wells Fargo & Co.	1.0 billion*
6	6	Jardine Lloyd Thompson Group Plc.	905.9 million
7	7	Brown & Brown Inc.	878.0 million
8	8	BB&T Insurance Services Inc.	876.5 million
9	10	Hilb Rogal & Hobbs Co.	710.8 million
10	14	Lockton Companies Inc.	667.0 million

*Because Wells Fargo is primarily a banking operation, it is ranked by brokerage revenue.

WHAT DOES IT MEAN?

BROKER: Insurance salesperson licensed as an agent and broker who acts as a go-between, searching the marketplace on behalf of the client for insurance coverage. Go to www.ambest.com/resource/glossary.html for a full glossary of insurance terms.

Public Insurers

GLOBAL INVESTING: These stock indexes reflect the trading patterns of equities issued by companies whose primary business is insurance.

WHAT BEST'S RATINGS MEAN: A Best's Financial Strength Rating is an independent opinion of an insurer's ability to meet its obligations to policyholders.

WHY A BEST'S RATING IS IMPORTANT: Insurance agents, brokers, financial advisers, banks and other insurance professionals utilize the ratings to determine an insurer's financial strength.

The 'AMB' vs. the 'DOW'

The AMB is comprised of insurance industry companies that are publicly traded, are listed on major global stock exchanges, and have an interactive Best's Rating.

(Year ended 6/28/2007) Index, Dec. 31, 2004 = 1000

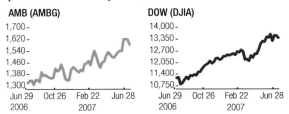

AMB (AMBG)

| 1,700 – |
| 1,620 – |
| 1,540 – |
| 1,460 – |
| 1,380 – |
| 1,300 |

Jun 29   Oct 26   Feb 22   Jun 28
2006   2007

DOW (DJIA)

| 14,000 – |
| 13,350 – |
| 12,700 – |
| 12,050 – |
| 11,400 – |
| 10,750 |

Jun 29   Oct 26   Feb 22   Jun 28
2006   2007

> **DID YOU KNOW?**
> **THE UNITED STATES** is the world's biggest insurance market. As of mid-2007, it employed 2.34 million people, according to the U.S. Bureau of Labor Statistics, up 9% from mid-1996.

Guide to Best's Financial Strength Ratings

Secure Ratings		What it Means
A++ and A+	Superior	1 in 1,667 companies in this category can be expected to fail.
A and A-	Excellent	1 in 500 companies in this category can be expected to fail.
B++, B+	Good	1 in 133 companies in this category can be expected to fail.
Vulnerable Ratings		**What it Means**
B and B-	Fair	1 in 48 companies in this category can be expected to fail.
C++ and C+	Marginal	1 in 29 companies in this category can be expected to fail.
C and C-	Weak	1 in 16 companies in this category can be expected to fail.
D	Poor	1 in 14 companies in this category can be expected to fail.
E	Under Regulatory Supervision	Not Applicable
F	In Liquidation	Not Applicable
S	Rating Suspended	Not Applicable

Note: The failure rates referenced in the table above are based on one-year cumulative average impairment rates.

Web extra: For information on issuer credit ratings and more: Go to *www.ambest.com*.

At the Market: Indexes by Region
Stock performance: A six-month look at composite indexes by region

(Six months ended 6/28/2007) Index, Dec. 31, 2004 = 1000

A.M. Best's U.S. Composite Insurance Index (AMBUS)

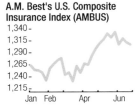

A.M. Best's European Insurance Index (AMBEUR)

A.M. Best's Asian/Pacific Insurance Index (AMBAP)

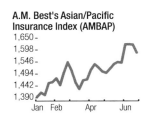

Multi-Line Indexes
Stock performance: A six-month look at Multi-Line indexes

(Six months ended 6/28/2007) Index, Dec. 31, 2004 = 1000

Web extra: Go to *www.ambest.com/stocks* for live market updates.

A.M. Best's U.S. Multi-Line Insurance Index (AMBUML)

A.M. Best's Global Multi-Line Insurance Index (AMBGML)

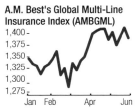

Top & Bottom Performers in the AMB
Six Months Ended June 30, 2007

	Top 10 Performers	Ticker	Currency	Closing Price	Six-month % Change
1	LIG Insurance Co. Ltd.	jd002550	KRW	22,650.00	57.29
2	Ohio Casualty Corp.	OCAS	USD	43.31	45.29
3	China Insurance International Holdings Co.	jB0966	HKD	14.22	45.10
4	Meritz Fire & Marine Insurance Co. Ltd.	jd000060	KRW	9,030.00	42.20
5	Hyundai Marine & Fire Insurance Co. Ltd.	jd001450	KRW	16,700.00	41.53
6	Converium Holding AG	eZCHRN	CHF	22.50	37.61
7	Atlantic American Corp.	AAME	USD	4.05	36.82
8	American National Insurance Co.	ANAT	USD	152.60	33.73
9	American Safety Insurance Holdings Ltd.	ASI	USD	23.83	28.46
10	Unum Group	UNM	USD	26.11	25.65
	Bottom 10 Performers				
1	KMG America Corp.	KMA	USD	5.25	-45.26
2	EMC Insurance Group Inc.	EMCI	USD	24.82	-27.26
3	Penn Treaty American Corp.	PTA	USD	5.72	-25.62
4	Donegal Group Inc.	DGICA	USD	14.90	-23.94
5	Safety Insurance Group Inc.	SAFT	USD	41.40	-18.36
6	Kingsway Financial Services Inc.	TKFS	CAD	19.96	-17.89
7	Alfa Corp.	ALFA	USD	15.57	-17.22
8	GAINSCO Inc.	GAN	USD	6.59	-16.90
9	Amlin PLC	ILAML	GBP	2.81	-13.68
10	CNA Surety Corp.	SUR	USD	18.91	-12.05

Sources: A.M. Best Co., Dow Jones Indexes.

Financial Controls

REPUTATION AND RISK: Insurance is one of the few industries that markets and sells products before the final cost is known. It is an industry that must rely on its best and brightest people to estimate costs.

SAFE AND SOUND: Insurers are required by law to have an independent certified public accountant approve their annual statutory audits. Why? Weak financial controls can contribute to inaccurate financial reporting, potentially resulting in fees, fines or loss of business.

Assuring Accuracy:
Top 10 Auditor Firms

Rank is based on insurance clients' net premiums written. ($ Millions)

PricewaterhouseCoopers
Deloitte
Ernst & Young
KPMG
BDO
Grant Thornton LLP
Strohm Ballweg LLP
Eide Bailly LLP
McGladrey & Pullen LLP
Johnson Lambert & Co.

0   50   100   150   200   250   300   350   400

Calculating Risks:
Top 10 Actuarial Firms

Rank is based on insurance clients' net premiums written. ($ Millions)

PricewaterhouseCoopers
Milliman
KPMG
Deloitte
Ernst & Young
Towers Perrin
Beneficial Consultants LLC
Reden & Anders Ltd.
Eckler Partners Ltd.
Oliver T Wilson Inc.

0   20   40   60   80   100

A.M. Best Special Report, "Insurance Auditors and Actuaries of North America" (1/1/07)

DID YOU KNOW?
THE TOP GLOBALLY TRADED INSURANCE STOCKS as of June 30, 2007—ranked by free-float market capitalization—were:

($ Billions)*

Rank	Country	Name	Ticker	Market Capitalization
1	US	American International Group Inc.	AIG	159.62
2	US	Berkshire Hathaway Inc.	BRK/A	112.93
3	DE	Allianz SE	eiALV	105.29
4	NL	ING Groep N.V.	eA30360	92.57
5	FR	AXA S.A.	eQ12062	77.68
6	US	UnitedHealth Group Inc.	UNH	68.89
7	US	Manulife Financial Corp.	MFC	57.72
8	US	WellPoint Inc.	WLP	49.48
9	IT	Assicurazioni Generali S.p.A.	eIG	48.53
10	US	Prudential Financial Inc.	PRU	46.57

* Free-Float market capitalization. Top stocks in A.M. Best Global Stock Index as of June 29, 2007.
Source: A.M. Best Co., Dow Jones Indexes.

Web extra: Go to A.M. Best's rating center at *www.ambest.com* for methodologies and further detail on Best's Ratings.

Who's New

Property/Casualty Companies Incorporated in 2006.

Company Name	AMB#	Location
Adirondack Insurance Exchange	13114	Williamsville, NY
Affirmative Insurance Company MI	13130	Bingham Farms, MI
AIX Specialty Insurance Co.	13763	Wilmington, DE
American Capital Assurance Corp.	13307	St. Petersburg, FL
Bristol West Preferred Ins. Co.	13761	Bingham Farms, MI
Catastrophe Reinsurance Co.	13592	San Antonio, TX
CUMIS Specialty Insurance Co.	13757	Waverly, IA
Direct Auto Insurance Co.	13774	Chicago, IL
FCCI Advantage Insurance Co.	13762	Sarasota, FL
First Acceptance Insurance Co. TN	13595	Nashville, TN
Hawaiian Insurance and Guaranty Co. Ltd	13317	Honolulu, HI
Knight Holdings Inc.	51975	Carson City, NV
Liberty Mutual Personal Ins. Co.	13107	Boston, MA
LightKeeper Insurance Co.	13570	Los Angeles, CA
MDOW Insurance Co.	13583	Houston, TX
Merchants National Insurance Co.	13588	Manchester, NH
PMI Guaranty Co.	13590	Jersey City, NJ
Prime Insurance Co.	13308	Chicago, IL
Public Title Insurance Co.	13116	Rochester, NY
Safe Harbor Insurance Co.	13123	Tallahassee, FL
Shelter Bay Insurance Co.	13316	Phoenix, AZ
Synergy Insurance Co.	13594	Charlotte, NC
Texas Heritage Insurance Co.	13135	Brenham, TX

Life/Health companies Incorporated in 2006.

Company Name	AMB#	Location
Arcadian Health Plan of GA Inc.	64888	Savannah, GA
Fidelis SecureCare of Texas	64860	Houston, TX
LifeSecure Insurance Co.	64869	Brighton, MI
PartnerCare Health Plan Inc.	64837	Tampa, FL
State Farm International Life Insurance Co. (Canada Branch)	66884	Aurora, ON
Tailwind Reinsurance Co.	60589	Columbia, SC
Timberlake Reinsurance Company II	60582	Charleston, SC
Trillium Community Health Plan	64863	Eugene, OR
UNICARE Health Plan of Kansas	64878	Topeka, KS
UNICARE Health Plan of South Carolina	64856	Columbia, SC
WellPath of South Carolina	64871	Columbia, SC

Web extra: Go to *www3.ambest.com/ccr* for a database on corporate changes and retirements.

Asset Distribution

THE "FLOAT" CYCLE: The interval between when the insurer receives a premium and the time a claim against that policy must be paid.
DURING THE CYCLE: The insurer invests the premium, making a profit or loss depending on how the investment performs.

Property/Casualty

Property/casualty insurance contracts are usually short-term — usually a year at most — whereas life and annuity contracts are long-term. In addition, the potential outcomes with property/casualty insurance contracts can vary widely, while claims against life insurance and annuity contracts are more predictable.

($ Billions)

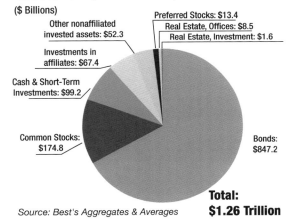

- Preferred Stocks: $13.4
- Real Estate, Offices: $8.5
- Real Estate, Investment: $1.6
- Other nonaffiliated invested assets: $52.3
- Investments in affiliates: $67.4
- Cash & Short-Term Investments: $99.2
- Common Stocks: $174.8
- Bonds: $847.2

Total: $1.26 Trillion

Source: Best's Aggregates & Averages

Life/Health
($ Billions)

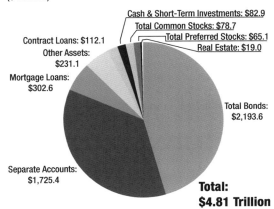

- Cash & Short-Term Investments: $82.9
- Total Common Stocks: $78.7
- Total Preferred Stocks: $65.1
- Real Estate: $19.0
- Contract Loans: $112.1
- Other Assets: $231.1
- Mortgage Loans: $302.6
- Total Bonds: $2,193.6
- Separate Accounts: $1,725.4

Total: $4.81 Trillion

Source: Best's Aggregates & Averages
Note: Totals may not add up due to rounding.

Mutual Insurance

CORPORATE STRUCTURE: An insurance company that is owned by its policyholders, who share in the company's surplus earnings.

OWNERS' RIGHTS: Policyholders have the ability to vote for the company's leadership, and also have a say in how net assets or surplus is distributed in the event the organization ceases to do business. The process in which a mutual company becomes a stock — or for-profit — company is referred to as demutualization.

CLOSE BUT NO CORPORATION: Resembling a mutual insurance company is a reciprocal insurance company. But whereas a mutual insurance company is incorporated, the reciprocal insurance company is run by a management company, also referred to as an attorney-in-fact.

Web extra: Read the Special Report: "Mutual Life Insurance Companies — Staying the Course" at *www.ambest.com*

Property/Casualty Mutuals vs. Life/Health Mutuals

Property/Casualty
2006 assets
$420.1 billion
2006 policyholder surplus
$157.5 billion

Life/Health
2006 assets
$747.6 billion*
2006 capital & surplus
$55.2 billion

Source: Best's Aggregates & Averages
Includes separate account business

Title Insurance

WHAT IT PROTECTS AGAINST: Insurance that covers a property owner from the risk that the title to real estate may contain defects, liens or encumbrances. Without a policy, a homeowner may not be fully protected against errors in the public records, hidden defects not disclosed by the public records, or mistakes made during the examination of the title of your new property.

Title Industry Revenue And Home Sales Activity
Title insurance revenues, mortgage rates and home sales.

	Total Operating Revenue ($ Millions)	30-Year Fixed Mortgage Yield (%)	Home Sales (Thousands)
1995	4,842.70	7.95	4,519
1996	5,552.20	7.80	4,924
1997	6,180.50	7.60	5,175
1998	8,276.80	6.94	5,852
1999	8,496.00	7.43	6,063
2000	7,869.20	8.06	6,051
2001	9,751.20	6.97	6,243
2002	12,625.90	6.54	6,605
2003	16,529.30	5.82	7,261
2004	16,377.30	5.84	7,982
2005	17,825.00	5.86	8,358

Source: A.M. Best Special Report, Strong Housing Market Drives Title Insurance Growth (11/27/2006)

DID YOU KNOW?
BENJAMIN FRANKLIN: diplomat, inventor, writer, insurer. The man of many interests and achievements was an incorporator of the first mutual insurance company in the United States in 1752. Called the Philadelphia Contributionship, the contributionship paid members to replace fire-damaged property.

Fiscal Fitness

BUSINESS INTERRUPTED:
When insurers become insolvent — the insurance world's rough equivalency of bankruptcy — the consequences can be dire for policyholders with outstanding claims against a failed company.

INSOLVENCY VS. BANKRUPTCY: The regulatory response to an insurer's financial impairment is distinct from bankruptcy proceedings that noninsurance companies undergo when they fail. The regulator in the troubled insurer's state of domicile may place the company under supervision or take other action to conserve the company's assets.

SAFETY NET: As a condition of doing business in most states, all insurance companies are members of a guaranty fund, or association. When there is a shortfall of funds needed to meet the obligations of policyholders, the remaining members in the state are assessed a share of the amount needed to meet the claims of policyholders in that state.

Primary Causes Of Property/Casualty Impairments

Over 38 years of A.M. Best impairment studies from 1969 to 2006, the dominant causes of impairment have remained constant: deficient loss reserves/inadequate pricing and rapid growth.

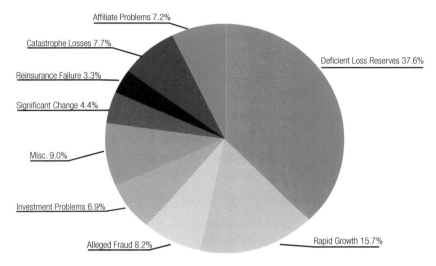

Source: A.M. Best Special Report, "15 Property/Casualty Insurers Identified as Impaired for 2006" (3/26/2007)

Primary Causes Of Life/Health Company Impairments

Impairment study results are influenced heavily by Accident & Health insurers, which have comprised roughly half of the population of impairments.

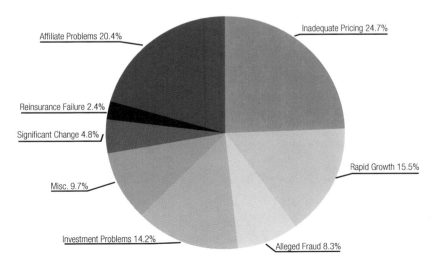

Source: A.M. Best Special Report, "Two Life/Health Insurance Impairments Identified for 2006; Trends Still Favorable" (3/26/2007)

Property/Casualty Insurance
Hitting home ... and business

WHAT PROPERTY/ CASUALTY INSURANCE PROTECTS AGAINST: Damage, loss or injury to the insured, as well as legal liability for damages caused to other people or their property.

LINES OF BUSINESS: The business, which includes auto, homeowners and commercial insurance, is one segment of the insurance industry. The other sector is life/health.

EVERYWHERE ELSE: Outside the United States, property/casualty insurance is referred to as nonlife or general insurance.

At the Market:
Property/Casualty & Nonlife
Stock performance: A six-month look at Property/Casualty & Nonlife.

(Six months ended 6/28/2007) Index, Dec. 31, 2004 = 1000

A.M. Best's U.S. Property/Casualty Insurance Index (AMBUPC)

A.M. Best's Global Nonlife Insurance Index (AMBGNL)

Source: A.M. Best, Dow Jones Indexes

DID YOU KNOW?

EACH U.S. INSURANCE COMPANY is domiciled in the state where it is incorporated or chartered. Just four states – Illinois, New York, Pennsylvania and Texas – were home in 2006 to more than 200 property/casualty companies, according to *Best's Key Rating Guide*, with New York leading the way with 237 companies.

Assets

Property owned by insurance companies — primarily stocks, bonds, mortgages and real estate.

Assets by Year

U.S. Industry ($ Trillions)

Top U.S. Property/Casualty Insurers

Assets 2006 ($ Billions)

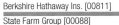

Berkshire Hathaway Ins. [00811]
State Farm Group [00088]
Amer Intl. Group Inc. [18540]
Travelers Group [18647]
Allstate Ins. Group [00008]
Liberty Mutual Ins. Cos. [00060]
CNA Ins. Cos. [18313]
Hartford Ins. Group [00048]
Nationwide Group [05987]
Chubb Group of Ins. Cos. [00012]

0   30   60   90   120   150

Source: A.M. Best Statistical Study (9/3/07)

Policyholder Surplus

The sum remaining after all liabilities are deducted from assets – essentially an insurer's net worth.

Policyholder Surplus

U.S. Industry ($ Billions)

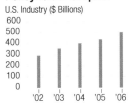

Top U.S. Property/Casualty Insurers

Policyholder Surplus 2006 ($ Billions)

Berkshire Hathaway Ins. [00811]
State Farm Group [00088]
Amer Intl. Group Inc. [18540]
Travelers Group [18647]
Allstate Ins. Group [00008]
Hartford Ins. Group [00048]
Nationwide Group [05987]
Liberty Mutual Ins. Cos. [00060]
USAA Group [04080]
Chubb Group of Ins. Cos. [00012]

0   10   20   30   40   50   60

Source: A.M. Best Statistical Study (9/3/07)

Premiums

Direct premiums written are before reinsurance transactions — insurance purchased by an insurance company to reduce risk. Net premiums are after the reinsurance deductions.

Net Premiums

U.S. Industry ($ Billions)

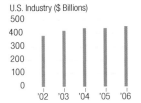

Top U.S. Property/Casualty Insurers

Direct Premiums Written 2006 ($ Billions)

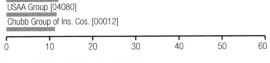

State Farm Group [00088]
Amer Intl. Group, Inc. [18540]
Allstate Ins. Group [00008]
Travelers Group [18647]
Liberty Mutual Ins. Cos. [00060]
Nationwide Group [05987]
Berkshire Hathaway Ins. [00811]
Farmers Ins. Group [00032]
Progressive Ins. Group [00780]
Hartford Ins. Group [00048]

0   10   20   30   40   50

Source: A.M. Best Statistical Study (4/2/07)

Catastrophes

PICKING UP THE PIECES: Catastrophe is the term used to describe a single or a series of related man-made or natural disasters that cause insured property losses of at least $25 million and affect a significant number of policyholders and insurers.

U.S. Catastrophes:
10 Largest Insured Property Losses

Ranked by losses restated into 2007 Dollars* ($ Billions)

Original ▨ 2007 Dollars

- Hurricane Katrina (2005)
- San Francisco Earthquake and Fire (1906)
- 9/11 Terrorist Attack (2001)
- Hurricane Andrew (1992)
- Northridge Earthquake (1994)
- Hurricane Wilma (2005)
- Great New England Hurricane (1938)
- Chicago Fire (1871)
- Hurricane Charley (2004)
- Hurricane Hugo (1989)

0   10   20   30   40

*Inflation adjustment 1908 to 2007 made using the Construction Cost Index (McGraw Hill) (2007 based on June), 1870 to 1907 based on CCI and overlapping CPI and McCusker inflation index (1860 to 1912).
Source: Insured losses estimates are from A.M. Best news archives and ISO/PCS.

Hurricanes

A WELCOME RESPITE: Following two years in which seven hurricanes generated insured losses that ranked them among the 13 most expensive storms ever, 2006 saw no hurricanes make landfall in the United States.

U.S. Hurricanes:
Largest Insured Property Losses
Ranked by losses restated into 2007 dollars* ($ Billions)

Rank	Hurricane	Year	Insured Losses
1	Hurricane Katrina	2005	43.7
2	Hurricane Andrew	1992	24.9
3	Hurricane Wilma	2005	11.1
4	Great New England Hurricane	1938	10.4
5	Hurricane Charley	2004	8.4
6	Hurricane Ivan	2004	8.0
7	Hurricane Hugo	1989	7.2
8	Hurricane Rita	2005	6.1
9	Hurricane Frances	2004	5.1
10	Miami Hurricane	1926	4.4
13	**Hurricane Jeanne**	**2004**	**3.9**

*Inflation adjustment 1908 to 2007 made using the Construction Cost Index (CCI) (McGraw Hill). CCI for 2007 based on April year/year growth.
Source: A.M. Best Special Report (5/21/2007)

Web extra: Go to *www.ambest.com* to read the entire 2007 Special Report: "U.S. Hurricane Catastrophe Review. One Blow Away from $6 Gas"

Tornadoes

NEW TORNADO ALLEY?
Surprise, New Jerseyans.
Most people associate tornadoes with the "Tornado Alley"
of the Great Plains states.
While this is true in terms
of the numbers of tornadoes
and losses, New Jersey tops
the list of states with the
highest average expected
insured losses per 1,000
square miles from tornado
and related weather events.

10 Costliest U.S. Tornadoes

Rank	Date	Location	Billions of 2007 Dollars*
1	Mar 31, 1973	Central-Northern Georgia	5.21
2	Jun 8, 1966	Topeka, Kansas	1.94
3	May 11 1970	Lubbock, Texas	1.43
4	May 3, 1999	Oklahoma City, Oklahoma	1.30
5	Apr 3, 1974	Xenia, Ohio	0.98
6	May 6, 1975	Omaha, Nebraska	0.91
7	Apr 10, 1979	Wichita Falls, Texas	0.73
8	Jun 3, 1980	Grand Island, Nebraska	0.70
9	Oct 3, 1979	Windsor Locks, Connecticut	0.66
10	May 8, 2003	Oklahoma City, Oklahoma	0.44

*Damages are total, not just insured property losses.
Sources: NOAA, A.M. Best Co. using Construction Cost Index deflator.
Source: A.M. Best Special Report (4/17/2007)

Damaging Tornado/Hail Events by State

Rank	State	Modeled Average Annual Loss ($ Mil) per 1,000**
1	NJ	15.70
2	CT	15.44
3	MA	13.54
4	OH	12.01
5	RI	11.41
6	MD	9.49
7	IL	8.61
8	OK	7.75
9	DE	7.23
10	IN	6.88

** 1,000 square miles is a
circular radius of 17.8 miles
Source: A.M. Best Special
Report (4/17/07)

Earthquakes

SOUND AND FURY:
The U.S. property/casualty
insurance industry is long
overdue for heavy losses
from a powerful earthquake.
The last such events that
caused wide-scale damage
in the United States were the
1994 Northridge Earthquake
in Los Angeles and the 1989
Loma Prieta quake in the
San Francisco Bay area. The
temblors each claimed more
than 60 lives.

U.S. Earthquakes:
Insured Property Loss of $1 Billion and More
Ranked by Loss Restated into 2006 Dollars*

Rank	Earthquake	Year	Magnitude	Insured Losses $ Billions
1	San Francisco Earthquake and Fire	1906	7.8	29.3
2	Northridge Earthquake	1994	6.7	17.8
3	Prince William Sound, Alaska, Earthquake and Tsunami	1964	9.2	4.1
4	San Fernando Earthquake	1971	6.5	2.7
5	Loma Prieta (San Francisco Bay Area)	1989	6.9	1.7

* Inflation adjustment made using the Construction Cost Index (CCI) (McGraw Hill).
Source: A.M. Best Special Report (10/2006)

Web extra: To read these special reports – "U.S. Tornadoes: Toto - We're Not In New Jersey Anymore,"
and "Annual Earthquake Study: $100 Billion of Insured Loss in 40 Seconds" – log onto *www.ambest.com*.

Asbestos & Environmental

Asbestos and Environmental losses continue to grow as the environmental risk with pollution liability presents a constant challenge to businesses. Companies increasingly face costly litigation, mandated cleanups and high court awards.

Mounting Losses

Top 10 groups with average annual incurred losses of at least $100 million per year ($ Thousands).

Rank	Groups	Total 5-Year Average Annual Incurred Loss
1	Travelers	$1,249,775
2	Hartford	663,999
3	ACE INA	441,105
4	AIG	429,271
5	CNA Ins Cos	399,895
6	Nationwide	317,420
7	Liberty Mutual	285,855
8	Allstate	262,650
9	Chubb Group	233,252
10	White Mountains	218,164

Source: A.M. Best Special Report, "Asbestos and Environmental Losses Rose During 2005 as Asbestos Funding Neared Completion" (4/2/2007)

Excess & Surplus

If property/casualty coverage isn't available from admitted insurers — ones licensed by a state — it can be be purchased from a nonadmitted carrier. The nonadmitted insurer escapes most regulation, and is free from some coverage requirements that apply to an admitted insurer.

Top U.S. Surplus Lines Groups

Direct Premium Written 2006 ($ Billions)

American International Group Inc. [18540]

Lloyd's [85202]

Zurich Financial Services NA Group [86976]

Nationwide Group [05987]

ACE INA Group [18498]

W. R. Berkley Group [04655]

Markel Corporation Group [18468]

Berkshire Hathaway Insurance Group [00811]

Alleghany Insurance Holdings [18640]

CNA Insurance Companies [18313]

0   2   4   6   8   10

Source: A.M. Best Special Report, "Surplus Lines Insurers Weather Soft Market with Profits Intact" (10/1/2007)

How Premiums Stack Up Between Surplus and Commercial Lines

A comparison over the past two decades of the growth in the surplus lines industry with that of the commercial lines industry. ($ Thousands).

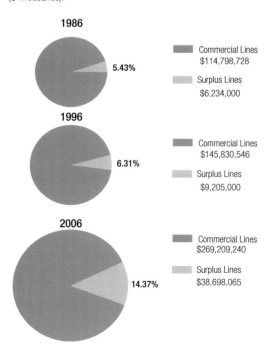

1986

5.43%

Commercial Lines $114,798,728

Surplus Lines $6,234,000

1996

6.31%

Commercial Lines $145,830,546

Surplus Lines $9,205,000

2006

14.37%

Commercial Lines $269,209,240

Surplus Lines $38,698,065

Lines of Business

FRONT OF THE LINES:

Auto coverage, homeowners and workers' compensation dominate mostly because those lines have common legal provisions that force drivers, homeowners and employers to obtain coverage.

U.S. Property/Casualty Direct Premiums Written 2006

Number in parenthesis represents the percentage change from 2005.
($ Billions)

96.0-	Private Passenger Auto Liability (0.3)
66.0-	Private Passenger Auto Physical Damage (0.4)
61.3-	Homeowners Multiple Peril (7.3)
53.8-	Workers' Compensation (-3.8)
53.3-	Other Liability (4.0)
35.6-	Commercial Multiple Peril (5.5)
22.3-	Commercial Auto Liability (0.0)
13.4-	Inland Marine (12.1)
11.5-	Medical Malpractice (-1.3)
10.8-	Fire (20.8)
10.1-	Allied (26.4)
7.5-	Commerical Auto Physical Damage (-0.5)
5.3-	Mortgage Guaranty (3.6)
4.95-	Surety (12.2)
4.9-	Multiple Peril Crop (25.3)
4.3-	Product Liability (2.1)
3.2-	Group Accident & Health (-34.0)
3.1-	Ocean Marine (9.8)
2.8-	Financial Guaranty (-6.8)
2.5-	Farmowners Multiple Peril (3.6)
2.4-	Earthquake (18.6)
2.3-	Federal Flood (19.9)
2.2-	Aircraft (5.6)
1.9-	Other Accident & Health (-19.9)
1.3-	Credit (15.0)
1.2-	Fidelity (-5.8)
1.1-	Boiler and Machinery (4.0)
0.2-	Burglary and Theft (61.1)

Source: A.M. Best Statistical Study (7/30/2007)

2006 Combined Ratios By Line of Business*

Number in parenthesis represents the 10-year combined ratio.

112.1-	Farmowners Multiple Peril (102.6)
111.2-	Federal Flood (188.9)
99.5-	Private Passenger Auto Liability (104.6)
99.3-	Commercial Multiple Peril - Liability (112.0)
98.6-	Ocean Marine (102.0)
94.6-	Workers' Compensation (109.5)
93.2-	Other Liability (113.7)
91.9-	Other Accident & Health (92.7)
90.9-	Commercial Auto Liability (106.0)
90.6-	Private Passenger Auto Physical Damage (94.5)
87.7-	Product Liability (168.0)
87.6-	Commercial Auto Physical Damage (94.0)
87.1-	Medical Malpractice (117.8)
85.9-	Homeowners Multiple Peril (103.0)
78.9-	Credit (87.2)
77.8-	Commercial Multiple Peril - Nonliability (101.0)
77.6-	Group Accident & Health (98.0)
76.7-	Multiple Peril Crop (95.0)
73.4-	Inland Marine (87.6)
70.7-	Fire (86.2)
70.1-	Fidelity (85.8)
68.8-	Surety (100.7)
68.4-	Boiler & Machinery (72.1)
67.1-	Allied (130.0)
64.0-	Mortgage Guaranty (59.0)
63.3-	Aircraft (85.9)
55.2-	Credit A&H (65.3)
52.6-	Burglary & Theft (59.4)
34.9-	Financial Guaranty (31.2)
28.8-	Earthquake (43.5)

* All references to combined ratio in this book are after dividend.
Source: Best's Aggregates & Averages

CATASTROPHE WEARY

THE SEPT. 11, 2001, terrorist attacks, and 2005's Hurricane Katrina wreaked havoc on insurers. The effects of these two events are readily evident in the majority of combined-ratio and premium spikes in certain individual property/casualty business lines.

WHAT DOES IT MEAN?

COMBINED RATIO: The percentage of premiums an insurer has to pay out in claims and expenses. If it is less than 100%, the company is making an underwriting profit.

All Auto

Automobile insurance is the most bought insurance in the United States. Different coverages can be purchased based on the needs of the insured.

Direct Premiums
U.S. Industry ($ Billions)

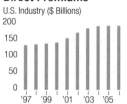

Combined Ratio
U.S. Industry

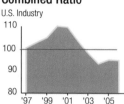

Top U.S. Writers
Direct Premiums Written 2006 ($ Billions)

State Farm Group [00088]
Allstate Insurance Group [00008]
Progressive Insurance Group [00780]
Berkshire Hathaway Insurance Group [00811]
Nationwide Group [05987]
Farmers Insurance Group [00032]
USAA Group [04080]
Liberty Mutual Insurance Companies [00060]
Travelers Insurance Companies [18674]
American International Group Inc. [18540]

Source: Best's Aggregates & Averages, Best's State/Line Database

Commercial Auto

Direct Premiums
U.S. Industry ($ Billions)

Combined Ratio
U.S. Industry

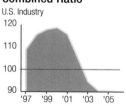

Top U.S. Writers
Direct Premiums Written 2006 ($ Billions)

Old Republic General Insurance Group [00734]
CNA Insurance Companies [18313]
Hartford Insurance Group [00048]
Travelers Insurance Companies [18674]
Progressive Insurance Group [00780]
Zurich Financial Services NA Group [18549]
Liberty Mutual Insurance Companies [00060]
American International Group Inc. [18540]
State Farm Group [00088]
Nationwide Group [05987]

Source: Best's Aggregates & Averages, Best's State/Line Database

Private Passenger

Direct Premiums
U.S. Industry ($ Billions)

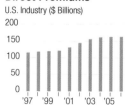

Combined Ratio
U.S. Industry

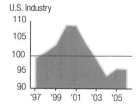

Top U.S. Writers
Direct Premiums Written 2006 ($ Billions)

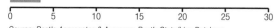

State Farm Group [00088]
Allstate Insurance Group [00008]
Progressive Insurance Group [00780]
Berkshire Hathaway Insurance Group [00811]
Farmers Insurance Group [00032]
Nationwide Group [05987]
USAA Group [04080]
Liberty Mutual Insurance Companies [00060]
American International Group Inc. [18540]
American Family Insurance Group [00124]

Source: Best's Aggregates & Averages, Best's State/Line Database

Other Liability

Liability insurance coverage protects against legal liability resulting from negligence, carelessness or a failure to act causing property damage or personal injury to others.

Top U.S. Writers

Direct Premiums Written 2006 ($ Billions)

American International Group Inc. [18540]
Zurich Financial Services NA Group [18549]
Travelers Insurance Companies [18674]
Chubb Group of Insurance Companies [00012]
ACE INA Group [18498]
CNA Insurance Companies [18313]
XL America Group [18130]
Liberty Mutual Insurance Companies [00060]
Nationwide Group [05987]
Hartford Insurance Group [00048]

0   2   4   6   8   10

Source: Best's Aggregates & Averages, Best's State/Line Database

Direct Premiums
U.S. Industry ($ Billions)

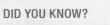

60
50
40
30
20
10
0
   '97 '99 '01 '03 '05

Combined Ratio
U.S. Industry

140
130
120
110
100
90
   '97 '99 '01 '03 '05

DID YOU KNOW?
TWO STATES – New Hampshire and Wisconsin – do not have compulsory auto insurance liability laws.

Workers' Compensation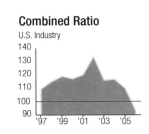

It is a system under which employers provide insurance — and the payment of lost wages — for employees in the case of injury, disability or death resulting from workplace hazards.

Top U.S. Writers

Direct Premiums Written 2006 ($ Billions)

American International Group Inc. [18540]
Liberty Mutual Insurance Companies [00060]
State Compensation Insurance Fund of CA [04028]
Travelers Insurance Companies [18674]
Hartford Insurance Group [00048]
Zurich Financial Services NA Group [18549]
State Insurance Fund of New York [04029]
ACE INA Group [18498]
Berkshire Hathaway Insurance Group [00811]
CNA Insurance Companies [18313]

0   1   2   3   4   5   6   7   8

Source: Best's Aggregates & Averages, Best's State/Line Database

Direct Premiums
U.S. Industry ($ Billions)

60
50
40
30
20
10
0
   '97 '99 '01 '03 '05

Combined Ratio
U.S. Industry

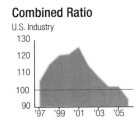

130
120
110
100
90
   '97 '99 '01 '03 '05

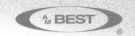

Commercial Multiple Peril Total

Commercial Multiple Peril policies protect the physical assets of large businesses as well as actions of owners or employee dishonesty that result in liability exposure.

Top U.S. Writers
Direct Premiums Written 2006 ($ Billions)

Travelers Insurance Companies [18674]
Hartford Insurance Group [00048]
Chubb Group of Insurance Companies [00012]
Nationwide Group [05987]
State Farm Group [00088]
Liberty Mutual Insurance Companies [00060]
Zurich Financial Services NA Group [18549]
CNA Insurance Companies [18313]
Farmers Insurance Group [00032]
Allianz of America Inc. [18429]

0.0   0.5   1.0   1.5   2.0   2.5   3.0   3.5

Source: Best's Aggregates & Averages, Best's State/Line Database

Direct Premiums
U.S. Industry ($ Billions)

Combined Ratio
U.S. Industry

Homeowners Multiple Peril

Typical policies cover most property or liability perils — such as fire or theft — to which the homeowner is exposed. Coverage includes structures on the property, as well as personal possessions in the structures.

Top U.S. Writers
Direct Premiums Written 2006 ($ Billions)

State Farm Group [00088]
Allstate Insurance Group [00008]
Farmers Insurance Group [00032]
Nationwide Group [05987]
Travelers Insurance Companies [18674]
USAA Group [04080]
Liberty Mutual Insurance Companies [00060]
Chubb Group of Insurance Companies [00012]
American Family Insurance Group [00124]
Citizens Property Insurance Corporation [11712]

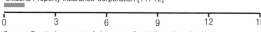

0   3   6   9   12   15

Source: Best's Aggregates & Averages, Best's State/Line Database

Direct Premiums
U.S. Industry ($ Billions)

Combined Ratio
U.S. Industry

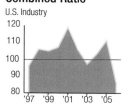

Farmowners Multiple Peril

Policies are similar to homeowners insurance, protecting farmowners and ranchowners against a number of named perils and liabilities. Coverage usually protects the home and its contents, as well as barns, stables and other structures.

Direct Premiums
U.S. Industry ($ Billions)

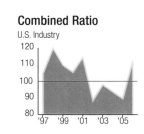

Combined Ratio
U.S. Industry

Top U.S. Writers
Direct Premiums Written 2006 ($ Millions)

Nationwide Group [05987]
State Farm Group [00088]
Farm Bureau Mutual Group [04233]
Travelers Insurance Companies [18674]
Country Insurance & Financial Services [00302]
American Family Insurance Group [00124]
Tennessee Farmers Insurance Companies [18154]
Kentucky Farm Bureau Group [03281]
United Farm Bureau of Indiana Group [04232]
White Mountains Insurance Group [18490]

0   50   100   150   200   250

Source: Best's Aggregates & Averages, Best's State/Line Database

Multiple Peril Crop

Crop insurance, written under the jurisdiction of the National Crop Insurance Services, covers growing crops against perils such as hail, wind and fire.

Direct Premiums
U.S. Industry ($ Billions)

Combined Ratio
U.S. Industry

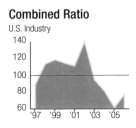

Top U.S. Writers
Direct Premiums Written 2006 ($ Millions)

ACE INA Group [18498]
Centurion Insurance Group [18188]
NAU Country Insurance Company [11098]
Allianz of America, Inc. [18429]
Great American P & C Insurance Grp. [04835]
American Agri-Business Insurance Company [12624]
Agri General Insurance Company [01935]
XL America Group [18130]
Producers Agriculture Insurance Group [18575]
Farmers Alliance Companies [00114]

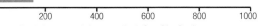

0   200   400   600   800   1000

Source: Best's Aggregates & Averages, Best's State/Line Database

Inland Marine

Coverage was developed for shipments that do not involve ocean transport. It covers articles in transit by all forms of land and air transportation as well as bridges, tunnels and other means of transportation and communication. It also provides special coverage for distinctive items such as jewelry, fine arts and silverware.

Top U.S. Writers

Direct Premiums Written 2006 ($ Millions)

American International Group Inc. [18540]
CNA Insurance Companies [18313]
Travelers Insurance Companies [18674]
Zurich Financial Services NA Group [18549]
FM Global Group [18502]
State Farm Group [00088]
Allianz of America Inc. [18429]
Liberty Mutual Insurance Companies [00060]
Assurant Solutions [18499]
Chubb Group of Insurance Companies [00012]

0   200   400   600   800   1,000   1,200

Source: Best's Aggregates & Averages, Best's State/Line Database

Direct Premiums
U.S. Industry ($ Billions)

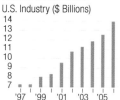

Combined Ratio
U.S. Industry

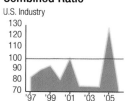

Ocean Marine

Ocean marine insures against property damage to all types of vessels and watercraft and to the loss of cargo. Coverage excludes war and terrorism risk.

Top U.S. Writers

Direct Premiums Written 2006 ($ Millions)

American International Group Inc. [18540]
Travelers Insurance Companies [18674]
ACE INA Group [18498]
CNA Insurance Companies [18313]
Allianz of America Inc. [18429]
American Steamship Owners Mut P & I Asn. [00161]
Chubb Group of Insurance Companies [00012]
White Mountains Insurance Group [18490]
XL America Group [18130]
Zurich Financial Services NA Group [18549]

0   50   100   150   200   250   300   350   400

Source: Best's Aggregates & Averages, Best's State/Line Database

Direct Premiums
U.S. Industry ($ Billions)

Combined Ratio
U.S. Industry

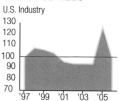

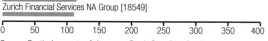

LANGUAGE PERIL

HOW CAN SOMETHING ON WATER BE INLAND? The meaning of the term "inland marine" in the United States can be a source of confusion. Historically, it was shaved off of ocean marine policies to cover the non-ocean portion of the journey. If you think of marine as meaning transporting over water, then think of transporting over land as inland marine.

Allied Lines

Think wind, rain and fire. Allied lines are types of property insurance that are usually bought in conjunction with fire insurance. It includes wind, water damage and vandalism coverage.

Direct Premiums
U.S. Industry ($ Billions)

Combined Ratio
U.S. Industry

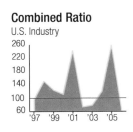

Top U.S. Writers

Direct Premiums Written 2006 ($ Billions)

Citizens Property Insurance Corporation [11712]
ACE INA Group [18498]
FM Global Group [18502]
Centurion Insurance Group [18188]
Allianz of America, Inc. [18429]
Travelers Insurance Companies [18674]
American International Group Inc. [18540]
NAU Country Insurance Company [11098]
Great American P & C Insurance Grp. [04835]
Fidelity National Group [18606]

0.0   0.5   1.0   1.5   2.0

Source: Best's Aggregates & Averages, Best's State/Line Database

Fire

Fire insurance protects property against losses caused by fire or lightning and usually is included in homeowners or commercial multiple peril policies.

Direct Premiums
U.S. Industry ($ Billions)

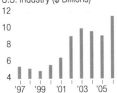

Combined Ratio
U.S. Industry

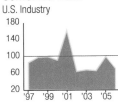

Top U.S. Writers

Direct Premiums Written 2006 ($ Billions)

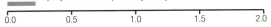

American International Group Inc [18540]
Travelers Insurance Companies [18674]
Assurant Solutions [18499]
FM Global Group [18502]
Zurich Financial Services NA Group [18549]
Liberty Mutual Insurance Companies [00060]
Alleghany Insurance Holdings [18640]
Farmers Insurance Group [00032]
Allianz of America Inc. [18429]
Citizens Property Insurance Corporation [11712]

0.0   0.5   1.0   1.5   2.0

Source: Best's Aggregates & Averages, Best's State/Line Database

Medical Malpractice

Policies provide professional liability coverage for physicians and other medical professionals against lawsuits alleging negligence or errors and omissions during the care of patients.

Direct Premiums
U.S. Industry ($ Billions)

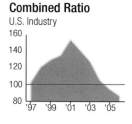

12
10
8
6
4

'97 '99 '01 '03 '05

Combined Ratio
U.S. Industry

160
140
120
100
80

'97 '99 '01 '03 '05

Top U.S. Writers
Direct Premiums Written 2006 ($ Millions)

MLMIC Group [18439]
American International Group Inc. [18540]
Berkshire Hathaway Insurance Group [00811]
ProAssurance Group [18559]
CNA Insurance Companies [18313]
Doctors Company Insurance Group [18083]
ISMIE Mutual Group [18644]
MAG Mutual Group [18635]
ProMutual Group [18359]
Physicians Reciprocal Insurers [02888]

0   200   400   600   800   1,000

Source: Best's Aggregates & Averages, Best's State/Line Database

Web extra: Read the 2007 special report - "U.S. Medical Malpractice Market Review: Medical Malpractice Sector Mends, But Remains Vulnerable To Cycles" - at *www.ambest.com.*

Mortgage Guaranty

Also called private mortgage insurance (PMI), mortgage guaranty insurance covers the lender originating the mortgage in the event that the mortgage holder defaults on a loan, spreading the risk of foreclosure between the lender and the insurer.

Direct Premiums
U.S. Industry ($ Billions)

6
5
4
3
2

'97 '99 '01 '03 '05

Combined Ratio
U.S. Industry

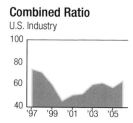

100
80
60
40

'97 '99 '01 '03 '05

Top U.S. Writers
Direct Premiums Written 2006 ($ Billions)

Mortgage Guaranty Group [03014]
Radian Group [18150]
American International Group Inc. [18540]
PMI Mortgage Group [03267]
Genworth PC Group [18694]
Old Republic General Insurance Group [00734]
Triad Guaranty Group [18374]
CMG Mortgage Insurance Company [02751]

0.0   0.3   0.6   0.9   1.2   1.5

Source: Best's Aggregates & Averages, Best's State/Line Database

---

BYE-BYE, PMI

THE FEDERAL "HOMEOWNERS' PROTECTION ACT" says that the PMI can be canceled when the mortgage has been paid down to 80% of the loan, and that it must automatically be canceled when the mortgage has been paid down to 78%.

Financial Guaranty

With financial guaranty insurance, losses from specified financial transactions are covered, and investors in debt instruments, such as municipal bonds, will receive timely principal and interest payments if a default occurs. It also hikes the credit rating of debt to which the guaranty is attached.

Top U.S. Writers

Direct Premiums Written 2006 ($ Millions)

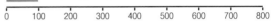

Ambac Financial Group [18449]
MBIA Group [03166]
Financial Security Assurance Group [04017]
Financial Guaranty Insurance Company [01859]
XL America Group [18130]
Radian Group [18150]
Assured Guaranty Corp [10916]

0   100   200   300   400   500   600   700   800

Direct Premiums
U.S. Industry ($ Billions)

Combined Ratio
U.S. Industry

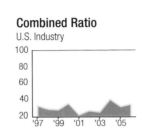

Source: Best's Aggregates & Averages, Best's State/Line Database

Product Liability

Coverage of the liability that parties along the supply chain of a product — from the manufacturer or the storeowner — has to assume if some defect in the product sold or manufactured injures a third party or damages his or her property.

Top U.S. Writers

Direct Premiums Written 2006 ($ Millions)

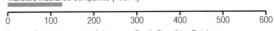

American International Group Inc [18540]
Zurich Financial Services NA Group [18549]
ACE INA Group [18498]
Chubb Group of Insurance Companies [00012]
W. R. Berkley Group [04655]
Liberty Mutual Insurance Companies [00060]
CNA Insurance Companies [18313]
Markel Corporation Group [18468]
Great American P & C Insurance Group [04835]
Travelers Insurance Companies [18674]

0   100   200   300   400   500   600

Direct Premiums
U.S. Industry ($ Billions)

Combined Ratio
U.S. Industry

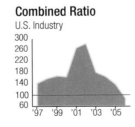

Source: Best's Aggregates & Averages, Best's State/Line Database

Fidelity

Coverage created to cover commercial businesses and financial establishments for losses of monies or stock through acts of employee dishonesty. Fidelity insurance must now encompass Internet transactions, as a dependence on e-commerce soars.

Direct Premiums
U.S. Industry ($ Billions)

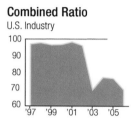

Combined Ratio
U.S. Industry

Top U.S. Writers
Direct Premiums Written 2006 ($ Millions)

Chubb Group of Insurance Companies [00012]
American International Group Inc. [18540]
Travelers Insurance Companies [18674]
Zurich Financial Services NA Group [18549]
CUMIS Insurance Society Group [18704]
Great American P & C Insurance Group [04835]
CNA Insurance Companies [18313]
Hartford Insurance Group [00048]
ACE INA Group [18498]
AXIS Insurance Group [18603]

0   50   100   150   200   250

Source: Best's Aggregates & Averages, Best's State/Line Database

Surety

Surety bonds guarantee that a principal will perform a specific obligation. They are three-party contracts:

The principal — the primary party who will be performing the obligation

The obligee — the party who is the recipient of the obligation

The surety — ensures that the obligation will be performed

In the case of public construction projects, surety bonds protect taxpayer dollars should the contractor default.

Top U.S. Writers
Direct Premiums Written 2006 ($ Millions)

Travelers Insurance Companies [18674]
Zurich Financial Services NA Group [18549]
CNA Insurance Companies [18313]
Safeco Insurance Companies [00078]
Chubb Group of Insurance Companies [00012]
Liberty Mutual Insurance Companies [00060]
Hartford Insurance Group [00048]
Arch Insurance Group [18484]
HCC Insurance Holdings [18421]
American International Group Inc. [18540]

0   200   400   600   800   1,000

Source: Best's Aggregates & Averages, Best's State/Line Database

Direct Premiums
U.S. Industry ($ Billions)

Combined Ratio
U.S. Industry

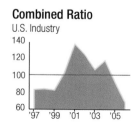

Aircraft

Insurers sell commercial airlines property insurance on the hulls and instrumentation of airplanes, and liability insurance for negligent acts that result in injury or property damage to passengers or others. Damage is covered on the ground and in the air. The policy limits the geographical area and individual pilots covered.

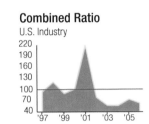

Direct Premiums
U.S. Industry ($ Billions)

Combined Ratio
U.S. Industry

Top U.S. Writers

Direct Premiums Written 2006 ($ Millions)

American International Group Inc. [18540]
Berkshire Hathaway Insurance Group [00811]
XL America Group [18130]
HCC Insurance Holdings [18421]
ACE INA Group [18498]
Old Republic General Insurance Group [00734]
Munich Re America Corporation Group [18259]
Liberty Mutual Insurance Companies [00060]
Zurich Financial Services NA Group [18549]
Allianz of America Inc. [18429]

Source: Best's Aggregates & Averages, Best's State/Line Database

Boiler & Machinery

Policies protect against a sudden or accidental breakdown of heating, cooling, production machinery and electrical equipment.

Direct Premiums
U.S. Industry ($ Billions)

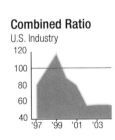

Combined Ratio
U.S. Industry

Top U.S. Writers

Direct Premiums Written 2006 ($ Millions)

FM Global Group [18502]
American International Group Inc. [18540]
Travelers Insurance Companies [18674]
Chubb Group of Insurance Companies [00012]
Zurich Financial Services NA Group [18549]
CNA Insurance Companies [18313]
Allianz of America Inc. [18429]
Nationwide Group [05987]
EMC Insurance Companies [00346]
Cincinnati Insurance Companies [04294]

Source: Best's Aggregates & Averages, Best's State/Line Database

Earthquake

Because earthquakes are not covered by standard homeowners or most business policies, coverage must be purchased separately. It covers direct damage to property resulting from an earthquake or volcano. It typically excludes damage resulting from fire, explosion, flood or a tidal wave that follows the quake or eruption.

Direct Premiums
U.S. Industry ($ Billions)

Combined Ratio
U.S. Industry

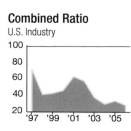

Top U.S. Writers
Direct Premiums Written 2006 ($ Millions)

California Earthquake Authority [12534]
State Farm Group [00088]
Zurich Financial Services NA Group [18549]
American International Group Inc. [18540]
GeoVera Insurance Group [25045]
AXIS Insurance Group [18603]
ACE INA Group [18498]
Travelers Insurance Companies [18674]
Endurance Specialty Group [18620]
ICW Group [02967]

Source: Best's Aggregates & Averages, Best's State/Line Database

Federal Flood

Like earthquake insurance, flood coverage is excluded under homeowners policies and many commercial property policies. Coverage for flood damage is available from the National Flood Insurance Program but is sold by licensed insurance agents.

Direct Premiums
U.S. Industry ($ Billions)

Combined Ratio
U.S. Industry

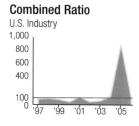

Top U.S. Writers
Direct Premiums Written 2006 ($ Millions)

Fidelity National Group [18606]
State Farm Group [00088]
Allstate Insurance Group [00008]
Hartford Insurance Group [00048]
Travelers Insurance Companies [18674]
Assurant Solutions [18499]
Selective Insurance Group [03926]
Nationwide Group [05987]
USAA Group [04080]
Farmers Insurance Group [00032]

Source: Best's Aggregates & Averages, Best's State/Line Database

Burglary & Theft

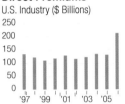

This is insurance for when someone breaks in and damages or steals your property at your home or while your business is closed. It is provided in a standard homeowners policy and in a business multiple peril policy.

Top U.S. Writers

Direct Premiums Written 2006 ($ Millions)

Liberty Mutual Insurance Companies [00060]
Travelers Insurance Companies [18674]
Chubb Group of Insurance Companies [00012]
Zurich Financial Services NA Group [18549]
Hartford Insurance Group [00048]
American International Group Inc. [18540]
Unitrin Inc. [05948]
Nationwide Group [05987]
CNA Insurance Companies [18313]
Sentry Insurance Group [00086]

0   10   20   30   40   50   60   70

Source: Best's Aggregates & Averages, Best's State/Line Database

Direct Premiums
U.S. Industry ($ Billions)

250
200
150
100
50
0

'97   '99   '01   '03   '05

Combined Ratio
U.S. Industry

100
88
76
64
52
40

'97   '99   '01   '03   '05

Credit

Credit insurance protects companies against the risk of non-payment by buyers arising from commercial risks, such as insolvency, or noncommercial risks, such as death, disability, or unemployment.

Top U.S. Writers

Direct Premiums Written 2006 ($ Millions)

Allianz of America Inc. [18429]
Allstate Insurance Group [00008]
American National P & C Group [18565]
Old Republic General Insurance Group [00734]
Stonebridge Casualty Insurance Company [00323]
Swiss Reinsurance Group [03262]
American International Group Inc. [18540]
Lyndon Property Insurance Company [03812]
Arch Insurance Group [18484]
White Mountains Insurance Group [18490]

0   50   100   150   200

Source: Best's Aggregates & Averages, Best's State/Line Database

Direct Premiums
U.S. Industry ($ Millions)

1500
1200
900
600
300
0

'97   '99   '01   '03   '05

Combined Ratio
U.S. Industry

120
110
100
90
80
70

'97   '99   '01   '03   '05

Assets

Canada's top property/casualty writers face the potential of a soft market cycle, especially if greater competition and looming reforms in the auto sector result in rate reductions.

Top Canada Property/Casualty Insurers

Assets 2006 (C$ Billions)

- ING Insurance Company of Canada [85758]
- Wawanesa Mutual Insurance Company [85802]
- Economical Mutual Insurance Company [85741]
- State Farm Mutual Automobile Ins. Company CAB [87096]
- The Nordic Insurance Company of Canada [85757]
- Co-Operators General Insurance Company [85735]
- Royal & Sun Alliance Ins. Company of Canada [85785]
- American Home Assurance Company CAB [86121]
- Aviva Insurance Company of Canada [85748]
- GE Capital Mortgage Insurance Company of CA [87757]

```
0     1     2     3     4     5     6     7     8
```
Source: Best's Aggregates & Averages

Capital & Surplus

As a battle for market share results heats up across Canada, financially flexible, more diversified companies with excess capital, or specialized companies with niches likely would not be hampered if market conditions worsen.

Top Canada Property/Casualty Insurers

Capital & Surplus 2006 (C$ Billions)

- Wawanesa Mutual Insurance Company [85802]
- GE Capital Mortgage Insurance Co. of CA [87757]
- State Farm Mutual Automobile Ins. Co. CAB [87096]
- Economical Mutual Insurance Company [85741]
- Co-Operators General Insurance Company [85735]
- ING Insurance Company of Canada [85758]
- The Nordic Insurance Company of Canada [85757]
- American Home Assurance Company CAB [86121]
- Security National Insurance Company [87089]
- Lloyds Underwriters CAB [87100]

```
0.0          0.5          1.0          1.5          2.0
```
Source: Best's Aggregates & Averages

Premiums

Despite a softening market, Canadian property/casualty insurers continued to post profitable underwriting results in 2006, with a net underwriting income of nearly C$2.8 billion on about C$30.8 billion of net premiums earned.

Top Canada Property/Casualty Insurers

Direct Premiums Written 2006 (C$ Billions)

- ING Insurance Company of Canada [85758]
- Wawanesa Mutual Insurance Company [85802]
- Economical Mutual Insurance Company [85741]
- Aviva Insurance Company of Canada* [85748]
- Co-Operators General Insurance Company [85735]
- State Farm Mutual Automobile Ins Co CAB [87096]
- Dominion of CA General Insurance Company [85739]
- Security National Insurance Company [87089]
- Zurich Insurance Company CAB [85148]
- American Home Assurance Company CAB [86121]

```
0.0    0.5    1.0    1.5    2.0    2.5    3.0    3.5
```
* Data purchased from Beyond 20/20
Source: A.M. Best Statistical Study

DID YOU KNOW?
MORE THAN two-thirds of Canada's property/ casualty insurance companies are domiciled in the province of Ontario, where one in three Canadians live, according to *Best's Key Rating Guide*.

Note:
* Financial data of Insurance Corporation of British Columbia, which was established in 1973 to provide universal auto insurance to B.C. motorists, is not included because it is run by the province.
*The data also excludes Lloyd's Underwriters Canada Branch due to significant differences between permitted and prescribed accounting practices.
(US$1 = C$1.1652 as of Dec. 31, 2006)

Auto

Despite underwriting gains, auto insurers saw their net loss ratio deteriorate to 67.6 in 2006 from 64.5 in 2005.

Top Canada P/C Insurers

Direct Premiums Written (C$ Billions)

ING Insurance Company of Canada [85758]
State Farm Mutual Automobile Insurance Company CAB [87096]
Wawanesa Mutual Insurance Company [85802]
Security National Insurance Company [87089]
Economical Mutual Insurance Company [85741]
Co-Operators Gen Insurance Company [85735]
Dominion of CA General Insurance Company [85739]
Aviva Insurance Company of Canada * [85748]
Pilot Insurance Company * [85779]
Unifund Assurance Company [86836]

0.0   0.5   1.0   1.5   2.0

Purchased data from Beyond 20/20
Source: A.M. Best Statistical Study (9/10/2007)

Commercial Property

Commercial property is the most profitable of the major lines, as a calmer 2006 followed a year that saw a major fire at the Suncor Oil Sands Facility and a series of severe storms wreak havoc on commercial businesses.

Top P/C Insurers

Direct Premiums Written (C$ Millions)

ING Insurance Company of Canada [85758]
Amer Home Assurance Company CAB [86121]
Aviva Insurance Company of Canada * [85748]
Zurich Insurance Company CAB [85148]
Commonwealth Insurance Company [85730]
Factory Mutual Insurance Company CAB [87010]
Lombard General Insurance Company of Canada [85732]
Economical Mutual Insurance Company [85741]
Co-Operators Gen Insurance Company [85735]
Royal & Sun Alliance Insurance CA [85785]

0   100   200   300   400   500

Purchased data from Beyond 20/20
Source: A.M. Best Statistical Study (9/10/2007)

Personal Property

The milder weather patterns in 2006 reduced the net loss ratio in personal property by 3.1 points to 65.2.

Web extra: Go to *www.ambest.com* for a look at A.M. Best's first-ever Review & Preview reports on Canadian Property/Casualty and Life.

Top Canada P/C Insurers

Direct Premiums Written 2006 (C$ Millions)

ING Insurance Company of Canada [85758]
Wawanesa Mutual Insurance Company [85802]
Co-Operators General Insurance Company [85735]
State Farm Fire & Casualty Company CAB [87095]
Economical Mutual Insurance Company [85741]
Security National Insurance Company [87089]
Dominion of CA General Insurance Company [85739]
Aviva Insurance Company of Canada * [85748]
Chubb Insurance Company of Canada [85725]
Pilot Insurance Company * [85779]

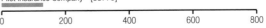

0   200   400   600   800

Purchased data from Beyond 20/20
Source: A.M. Best Statistical Report (9/10/2007)

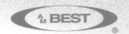

Life Insurance
It's Your Life – Be Prepared

A FINANCIAL GUARANTEE: Life insurance policies cover insureds and beneficiaries from the financial ravages of death, disability, frailty, and even from living too long.

Life insurance – pays a death benefit free from federal income tax that can be used to replace lost income or to pay estate taxes.

Disability insurance – provides an income when an insured cannot work because of disease or injury.

Long-term-care insurance – pays for skilled nursing, intermediate care, or custodial care for a patient in a nursing facility or residence.

OPPOSITE OF LIFE INSURANCE: Annuities — which can be used as a hedge against outliving assets — provide an income for life, a specified number of years, or a combination of the two.

PERMANENT VS. TERM: Permanent insurance uses higher premiums to build up cash in the policy that will pay for the insurance later in life when coverage becomes expensive. Term insurance lasts for a specified time, and yields a greater benefit for the premium dollar, but expires without value if the insured survives the specified period.

U.S. Life/Health Premiums: All Lines

Direct Premiums Written 2006 ($ Billions)

Individual Annuities
Ordinary Life
Group Annuities
Group Accident & Health
Other Accident & Health
Group Life
Credit Life
Credit Accident & Health

0   50   100   150   200

Source: Best's Aggregates & Averages

At the Market: Life

Stock performance: A six-month look at Life.
(Six months ended 6/28/2007) Index, Dec. 31, 2004 = 1000

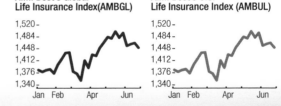

A.M. Best's Global
Life Insurance Index(AMBGL)

1,520 –
1,484 –
1,448 –
1,412 –
1,376 –
1,340 –

Jan Feb   Apr   Jun

A.M. Best's U.S.
Life Insurance Index (AMBUL)

1,520 –
1,484 –
1,448 –
1,412 –
1,376 –
1,340 –

Jan Feb   Apr   Jun

Admitted Assets

Admitted assets are those recognized and accepted by state insurance laws in determining solvency. State insurance laws prohibit companies from listing certain primary assets — such as accounts receivable that are over 90 days in arrears and office equipment — on its balance sheets.

Admitted Assets
U.S. Industry ($ Trillions)

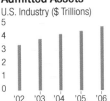

Top U.S. Life/Health Writers

Admitted Assets 2006 ($ Billions)

Metropolitan Life & Affiliated Cos. [70192]
Prudential of America Group [70189]
AIG Life Group [70342]
Hartford Life Group [70116]
Manulife Financial [69542]
TIAA Group [70362]*
AEGON USA Inc. [69707]
New York Life Group [69714]
ING USA Life Group [70153]
Axa Financial Group [70194]

0   100   200   300   400   500

TIAA's assets are significantly understated. Most of its separate account assets are in its affiliate, CREF.

Capital & Surplus

Capital and surplus is the sum remaining after liabilities are deducted from all assets — essentially an insurer's net worth.

Capital & Surplus
U.S. Industry ($ Billions)

Top U.S. Life/Health Writers

Capital & Surplus 2006 ($ Billions)

AIG Life Group [70342]
Metropolitan Life & Affiliated Cos. [70192]
TIAA Group [70362]
Northwestern Mutual Group [69515]
New York Life Group [69714]
MassMutual Financial Group [69702]
ING USA Life Group [70153]
Prudential of America Group [70189]
State Farm Life Group [70126]
Manulife Financial [69542]

0   5   10   15   20

Source: Best's Aggregates & Averages

Premiums

The amount of money a policyholder is charged for an insurance policy.

Direct Premiums
U.S. Industry ($ Billions)

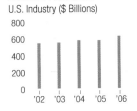

Top U.S. Life/Health Writers

Net Premiums Written 2006 ($ Billions)

Metropolitan Life & Affiliated Cos. [70192]
AIG Life Group [70342]
Prudential of America Group [70189]
UnitedHealth Group [69973]
Hartford Life Group [70116]
ING USA Life Group [70153]
Lincoln Financial Corp. [70351]
Manulife Financial [69542]
Axa Financial Group [70194]
New York Life Group [69714]

0   10   20   30   40   50

Source: Best's Aggregates & Averages

Individual Annuities

An individual annuity is an insurance product that makes periodic payments to individuals for a specific period of time or over the course of the individual's lifetime.

Deferred annuities: A type of long-term personal retirement account that allows assets to grow tax deferred until payment.

Immediate annuities: Annuities designed to guarantee owners a determined income stream on a monthly, quarterly, annual or semi-annual basis in exchange for a lump sum.

Top U.S. Writers

Net Premiums Written 2006 ($ Billions)

Metropolitan Life & Affiliated [70192]
Hartford Life Group [70116]
AIG Life Group [70342]
Lincoln Financial Group [70351]
Ameriprise Financial Group [69689]
Allianz Insurance Group [70187]
Pacific Life Group [69720]
Jackson National Group [69578]
TIAA Group [70362]
Prudential of America Group [70189]

Source: Best's Aggregates & Averages

Direct Premiums
U.S. Industry ($ Billions)

Group Annuities

Group annuities differ slightly from individual annuities in that the payout is dependent upon the life expectancy of all members of the group rather than on the individual.

Direct Premiums
U.S. Industry ($ Billions)

Top U.S. Writers

Net Premiums Written 2006 ($ Billions)

Prudential of America Group [70189]
ING USA Life Group [70153]
Manulife Finanical [69542]
AXA Financial Group [70194]
Metropolitan Life & Affiliated [70192]
AIG Life Group [70342]
MassMutual Financial Group [69702]
Hartford Life Group [70116]
AEGON USA Group [69707]
Great-West Life Group [70366]

Source: Best's Aggregates & Averages

DID YOU KNOW?

WITH 164 COMPANIES, TEXAS was home to more life/ health insurers than any other state in 2006, according to Best's Key Rating Guide. California was next with 155, followed by Pennsylvania, with 114, and New York, with 104.

Term Life

Term life insurance provides protection for a specified period of time. It pays a benefit only if the insured's death occurs during the coverage period.

Top U.S. Writers
Face Amount Issued 2006 ($ Billions)

AIG Life Group [70342]
Genworth Financial Group [69555]
State Farm Life Group [70126]
Primerica Group [70183]
Northwestern Mutual Group [69515]
Protective Life Corp. [69728]
Prudential of America Group [70189]
Metropolitan Life & Affiliated Cos. [70192]
Allstate Financial [70106]
New York Life Group [69714]

0   30   60   90   120   150

Top U.S. Writers
Face Amount In Force 2006 ($ Trillions)

Metropolitan Life & Affiliated Cos. [70192]
Swiss Reinsurance Group [70176]
AEGON USA Group [69707]
Scottish Re Group [70418]
ING USA Life Group [70153]
Lincoln Financial Group [70351]
Munich American Reassurance Co. [06746]
AIG Life Group [70342]
Genworth Financial Group [69555]
Primerica Group [70183]

0.0   0.5   1.0   1.5   2.0

Source: A.M. Best Statistical Studies (8/13/2007 & 8/24/2007)

Total Life

The size of a life insurance company often is measured by the face amount of its portfolio, that is, the amount of life insurance it has issued that is in force. Issued measures the face amount of the portfolio of policies an insurer has sold within a given time period.

WHAT DOES IT MEAN?
IN FORCE is that time before a policy premium matures and must be paid out or the policy expires because the policyowner doesn't pay up.

Top U.S. Writers
Face Amount Issued 2006 ($ Billions)

Metropolitan Life & Affiliated Cos. [70192]
AIG Life Group [70342]
Prudential of America Group [70189]
Hartford Life Group [70116]
Northwestern Mutual Group [69515]
Genworth Financial Group [69555]
State Farm Life Group [70126]
Protective Life Corp. [69728]
New York Life Group [69714]
Lincoln Financial Group [70351]

0   50   100   150   200   250

Top U.S. Writers
Face Amount In Force 2006 ($ Trillions)

Metropolitan Life & Affiliated Cos. [70192]
Prudential of America Group [70189]
Swiss Reinsurance Group [70176]
AEGON USA Group [69707]
ING USA Life Group [70153]
AIG Life Group [70342]
Lincoln Financial Group [70351]
Northwestern Mutual Group [69515]
New York Life Group [69714]
Hartford Life Group [70116]

0   1   2   3   4   5

Source: A.M. Best Statistical Studies (8/13/2007 & 8/24/2007)

Group Life

These life insurance policies are written for a group of members, most often employees, provided the group is not formed for the purpose of buying insurance. The cost per covered member is usually lower than purchasing individual policies.

Top U.S. Writers

Face Amount Issued 2006 ($ Billions)

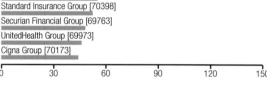

Metropolitan Life & Affiliated Cos. [70192]
Prudential of America Group [70189]
Hartford Life Group [70116]
Aetna Inc. [70202]
Unum Group [69743]
ING USA Life Group [70153]
Standard Insurance Group [70398]
Securian Financial Group [69763]
UnitedHealth Group [69973]
Cigna Group [70173]

0   30   60   90   120   150

Top U.S. Writers

Face Amount In Force 2006 ($ Trillions)

Metropolitan Life & Affiliated Cos. [70192]
Prudential of America Group [70189]
Hartford Life Group [70116]
Unum Group [69743]
Securian Financial Group [69763]
Aetna Inc. [70202]
ING USA Life Group [70153]
Cigna Group [70173]
Standard Insurance Group [70398]
New York Life Group [69714]

0.0   0.5   1.0   1.5   2.0   2.5

Source: A.M. Best Statistical Studies (8/13/2007 & 8/24/2007), Best's Aggregates and Averages

Direct Premiums

U.S. Industry ($ Billions)

40
35
30
25
20
15
10
5
0
'97 '99 '01 '03 '05

WHAT DOES IT MEAN?
NONFORFEITURE VALUE, also called cash surrender value, is the sum of money an insurance company will pay a policyholder if he or she decides to cancel the policy before it expires or before he or she dies.

Ordinary Life

Ordinary life insurance is issued in multiples of $1,000, with premiums payable continuously until the insured dies. Ordinary life policies can build up nonforfeiture values.

Direct Premiums

U.S. Industry ($ Billions)

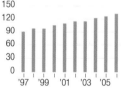

150
120
90
60
30
0
'97 '99 '01 '03 '05

Top U.S. Writers

Face Amount Issued 2006 ($ Billions)

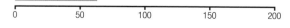

AIG Life Group [70342]
Northwestern Mutual Group [69515]
State Farm Life Group [70126]
Genworth Financial Group [69555]
Protective Life Corp. [69728]
Metropolitan Life & Affiliated Cos. [70192]
New York Life Group [69714]
Primerica Group [70183]
Prudential of America Group [70189]
Allstate Financial [70106]

0   50   100   150   200

Top U.S. Writers

Face Amount In Force 2006 ($ Trillions)

Metropolitan Life & Affiliated Cos. [70192]
Swiss Reinsurance Group [70176]
AEGON USA Group [69707]
Northwestern Mutual Group [69515]
Lincoln Financial Group [70351]
AIG Life Group [70342]
ING USA Life Group [70153]
Prudential of America Group [70189]
Scottish Re Group [70418]
Protective Life Corp. [69728]

0.0   0.5   1.0   1.5   2.0   2.5

Source: A.M. Best Statistical Studies (8/13/2007 & 8/24/2007), Best's Aggregates and Averages

Credit Life

Credit life insurance pays a borrower's outstanding balance on a specific loan or line of credit, up to the plan maximum, in the event the borrower dies before the balance is paid off.

Direct Premiums
U.S. Industry ($ Billions)

Top U.S. Writers
Face Amount Issued ($ Billions)

CUNA Mutual Group [70262]
Assurant [70135]
Protective Life Corp. [69728]
AIG Life Group [70342]
Citi Assurance Services Group [70434]
Aegon USA Group [69707]
HSBC Insurance Group [69620]
American National Group [70166]
Life of the South Group [69913]
Securian Financial Group [69763]

0   5   10   15   20

Top U.S. Writers
Net Premiums Written 2006 ($ Millions)

CUNA Mutual Group [70262]
AIG Life Group [70342]
HSBC Insurance Group [69620]
Citi Assurance Services Group [70434]
Securian Financial Group [69763]
Assurant [70135]
AEGON USA Group [69707]
American National Group [70166]
JMIC Life Group [69852]
Central States H&L Group [70363]

0   50   100   150   200   250

Top U.S. Writers
Face Amount In Force ($ Billions)

CUNA Mutual Group [70262]
AIG Life Group [70342]
Assurant [70135]
HSBC Insurance Group [69620]
AEGON USA Group [69707]
Citi Assurance Services Group [70434]
Securian Financial Group [69763]
Metropolitan Life & Affiliated Cos. [70192]
Amer National Group [70166]
Protective Life Corp. [69728]

0   5   10   15   20   25   30   35   40

Source: A.M. Best Statistical Studies (8/13/2007 & 8/24/2007), Best's Aggregates and Averages

---

Industrial Life

These low-value life insurance policies generally sell in amounts of less than $1,000. The premiums are collected by the salesperson on a weekly or monthly basis at the home of the insured.

Direct Premiums
U.S. Industry ($ Millions)

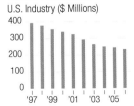

Top U.S. Writers
Net Premiums Written 2006 ($ Millions)

Metropolitan Life & Affiliated [70192]
Western & Southern Financial Group [69754]
Prudential of America Group [70189]
Unitrin Life & Health Group [70340]
AIG Life Group [70342]
Citizens Inc. Group [69688]
Security National Life Group [70382]
Mutual of Detroit Ins. Co. [06309]
Pan-American Life Group [69617]
Liberty Life Insurance Company [06175]

0   10   20   30   40   50

Source: Best's Aggregates & Averages

Credit Accident & Health

Insurance that covers a borrower for accidental injury, disability and related health expenses, and provides a monthly income.

Direct Premiums
U.S. Industry ($ Billions)

Top U.S. Writers
Net Premiums Written 2006 ($ Millions)

CUNA Mutual Group [70262]
Citi Assurance Services Group [70434]
HSBC Insurance Group [69620]
Securian Financial Group [69763]
Assurant [70135]
AIG Life Group [70342]
AEGON USA Group [69707]
Central States H&L Group [70363]
American National Group [70166]
Combined A&H Group [70178]

Source: Best's Aggregates & Averages

Group Accident & Health

These plans are designed for a natural group, such as employees of a single employer, or union members, and their dependents. Insurance is provided under a single policy, with individual certificates issued to each participant.

Direct Premiums
U.S. Industry ($ Billions)

Top U.S. Writers
Net Premiums Written 2006 ($ Millions)

UnitedHealth Group [69973]
Aetna Group [70202]
CIGNA Group [70173]
WellPoint Group [70064]
Metropolitan Life & Affiliated [70192]
Guardian Life [69685]
Hartford Life Group [70116]
Humana Group [69866]
Unum Group [69743]
Principal Life Insurance Co. [06150]

Source: Best's Aggregates & Averages

Other Accident & Health

Accident & Health policies do not cover sickness. Products that fall into this category could be policies that cover major medical, disability insurance, long-term-care, dental, dread disease or auxiliary coverages such as Medicare supplement.

Direct Premiums
U.S. Industry ($ Billions)

Top U.S. Writers
Net Premiums Written 2006 ($ Millions)

Aflac Incorporated Group [69824]
UnitedHealth Group [69973]
Humana Group [69866]
AIG Life Group [70342]
WellPoint Group [70064]
Unum Group [69743]
Conseco Insurance Group [69862]
Genworth Financial Group [69555]
Combined A&H Group [70178]
Torchmark Group [70265]

Source: Best's Aggregates & Averages

Assets

Canada life insurers had assets of C$276 at year end 2006, up from C$260 billion a year earlier.

Top Canada Life Insurers

Assets 2006 (C$ Billions)

Sun Life Assurance Company of Canada [07101]

Manufacturers Life Insurance Company [06688]

Great-West Life Assurance Company [06493]

London Life Insurance Company [06667]

Canada Life Assurance Company [06183]

Standard Life Assurance Co. of Canada [66846]

Industrial Alliance Ins. & Financial Svcs. [06554]

Munich Reinsurance Company CAB [66862]

Transamerica Life Canada [66805]

Independent Order of Foresters [60132]

| 0 | 10 | 20 | 30 | 40 | 50 | 60 | 70 | 80 |

Source: Best's Aggregates & Averages

Capital & Surplus

Recently, the Canadian life insurance industry has undergone changes including demutualization and consolidation. Currently, global operations have become important to Canada's top three life insurers, as a larger portion of revenue and earnings has come from business produced outside of Canada.

Top Canada Life Insurers

Capital & Surplus 2006 (C$ Billions)

Manufacturers Life Insurance Company [06688]

Great-West Life Assurance Company [06493]

Sun Life Assurance Company of Canada [07101]

Canada Life Assurance Company [06183]

London Life Insurance Company [06667]

Industrial Alliance Ins. & Financial Svcs. [06554]

Munich Reinsurance Company CAB [66862]

Metropolitan Life Insurance Co. CAB [69336]

RBC Life Insurance Company [66806]

Transamerica Life Canada [66805]

| 0 | 3 | 6 | 9 | 12 | 15 |

Source: Best's Aggregates & Averages

Premiums

The top three life insurance companies, known as "the big three," generated approximately two-thirds of the industry's 2006 net premium written.

Top Canada Life Insurers

Net Premiums Written 2006 (C$ Billions)

Sun Life Assurance Company of Canada [07101]

Manufacturers Life Insurance Company [06688]

Great-West Life Assurance Company [06493]

London Life Insurance Company [06667]

Munich Reinsurance Company CAB [66862]

Industrial Alliance Ins. & Financial Svcs. [06554]

Standard Life Assurance Co. of Canada [66846]

Canada Life Assurance Company [06183]

RBC Life Insurance Company [66806]

Co-operators Life Insurance Company [06290]

| 0 | 2 | 4 | 6 | 8 | 10 |

Source: Best's Aggregates & Averages

Group Life

Strong growth in premium from group and individual lines of business helped drive a 7% growth in premium income in 2006 over 2005.

Top Canada Writers

Net Premiums Written 2006 (C$ Billions)

Sun Life Assurance Company of Canada [07101]
Manufacturers Life Insurance Company [06688]
Munich Reinsurance Company (Canada Branch) [66862]
Great-West Life Assurance Company [06493]
Co-operators Life Insurance Company [06290]
London Life Insurance Company [06667]
Industrial Alliance Insurance & Financial Services Inc. [06554]
Industrial-Alliance Pacific Life Insurance Company [06838]
Canada Life Assurance Company [06183]
CUMIS Life Insurance Company [08815]

0.0   0.2   0.4   0.6   0.8   1.0   1.2

Source: A.M. Best Statistical Study (9/24/2007)

Individual Life

More Canadians may turn to individual health products as debate continues over how future costs will affect the financial well-being of the country's public health system, and calls for a parallel private health-care system get louder.

Top Canada Writers

Net Premiums Written 2006 (C$ Billions)

Sun Life Assurance Company of Canada [07101]
Manufacturers Life Insurance Company [06688]
London Life Insurance Company [06667]
Industrial Alliance Insurance & Financial Services Inc. [06554]
Munich Reinsurance Company (Canada Branch) [66862]
Canada Life Assurance Company [06183]
Transamerica Life Canada [66805]
RBC Life Insurance Company [66806]
Great-West Life Assurance Company [06493]
Canada Life Insurance Company [66839]

0.0   0.5   1.0   1.5   2.0   2.5   3.0   3.5   4.0

Source: A.M. Best Statistical Study (9/24/2007)

2006 Canadian Life Industry Investments

The Canadian investment environment continues to be healthy, but the high number of defaults in the U.S. subprime mortgage market has caused ripples. Investors' confidence has been somewhat shaken, even though Canada's subprime market makes up less than 10% of the mortgage market.

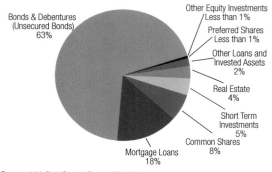

Bonds & Debentures (Unsecured Bonds) 63%
Other Equity Investments Less than 1%
Preferred Shares Less than 1%
Other Loans and Invested Assets 2%
Real Estate 4%
Short Term Investments 5%
Common Shares 8%
Mortgage Loans 18%

Source: A.M. Best Special Report (9/10/2007)

DID YOU KNOW?
OF THE 95 LIFE/HEALTH INSURERS domiciled in Canada in 2006, Ontario has 77 of them, according to *Best's Key Rating Guide.*

Health Insurance
Your Well-Being

HOW HEALTH INSURANCE WORKS: Policies pay benefits to insureds who become ill or injured.

Disability income insurance — Pays for loss of income due to disability

Medical expense insurance — Pays for hospital, doctor and other medical expenses

POLICY RISE: Managed care — which became very popular in the 1990s — is today the most common delivery system for health insurance. It is a system that controls the financing and delivery of health services through fee agreements with medical professionals and facilities to members enrolled in a specific plan.

Major types
- Health Maintenance Organizations (HMO)
- Preferred Provider Organizations (PPO)
- Point-of-service plans (POS)

HEALTH-CARE CHOICES: The 2003 Medicare Modernization Act allows individuals to combine a pretax savings account with a high-deductible health plan to establish a health savings account. The HSA pays for qualified and routine health-care expenses with tax-free money until you've met the deductible; then your insurance coverage takes over.

At the Market:
Health/HMO

Stock performance: A six-month look at Health/HMO

(Six months ended 6/28/2007)
Index, Dec. 31, 2004 = 1000

A.M. Best's U.S. Health & HMO Insurance Index (AMBUH)

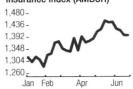

At the Market:
Life & Health/HMO

Stock performance: A six-month look at Life & Health/HMO

(Six months ended 6/28/2007)
Index, Dec. 31, 2004 = 1000

A.M. Best's U.S. Life/Health Insurance Index (AMBULH)

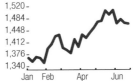

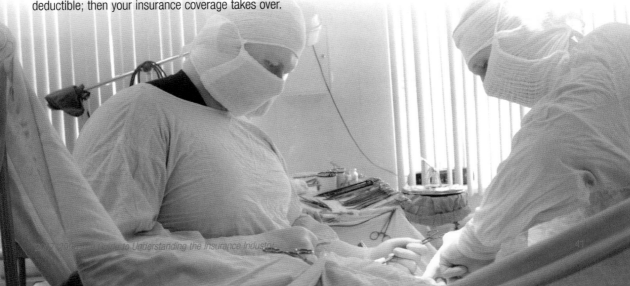

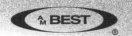

Financial

Total Revenue

In 2006, overall total revenues grew by 30.8% to $225 billion.
($ Billions) ■ 12/31/05 ■ 12/31/06

The implementation of Medicare Part D and Medicare Advantage plans fueled significant membership and revenue growth in 2006 for many health insurers. Over the long term, however, insurers — particularly those with a large percentage of enrollees in Medicare programs — could face financial implications if there is any reduction in Medicare funding by the government.

Aetna Inc.

AMERIGROUP Corp.

Centene Corp.

CIGNA HealthCare Inc.

Coventry Health Care Inc.

Health Net Inc.

Humana Inc.

Molina Healthcare Inc.

Sierra Health Services Inc.

UnitedHealth Group

WellCare Health Plans Inc.

WellPoint Inc.

0   10   20   30   40   50   60   70   80

Medical Loss Ratio

The average medical loss ratio increased by 90 basis points to 81.3 in 2006. (Medicare and Medicaid lines of business tend to have higher loss ratios and lower profit margins than commercial lines.)
(Percent)
■ 12/31/05 ■ 12/31/06

Aetna Inc.

AMERIGROUP Corp.

Centene Corp.

CIGNA HealthCare Inc.

Coventry Health Care Inc.

Health Net Inc.

Humana Inc.

Molina Healthcare Inc.

Sierra Health Services Inc.

UnitedHealth Group

WellCare Health Plans Inc.

WellPoint Inc.

70   75   80   85   90

Enrollment

Membership at publicly traded health insurance companies grew by 18 million, or 17.2%, in 2006.

(Millions) ■ 12/31/05 ■ 12/31/06

Aetna Inc.

AMERIGROUP Corp.

Centene Corp.

CIGNA HealthCare Inc.

Coventry Health Care Inc.

Health Net Inc.

Humana Inc.

Molina Healthcare Inc.

Sierra Health Services Inc.

UnitedHealth Group

WellCare Health Plans Inc.

WellPoint Inc.

0   5   10   15   20   25   30   35   40

Web extra: Go to *www.ambest.com* to read a variety of health-related reports, including the 12-month financial review: "Medicare Drove Health Plans' Growth as M&A Climate Cooled in 2006"

Source: A.M. Best Special Report (5/14/2007)

Blue Cross and Blue Shield Plans

The 38 Blue Cross and Blue Shield Plans are independent and locally owned and operated companies. Together, they comprise the nation's oldest and largest family of health benefit companies, now covering more than 94 million people.

For-Profit vs. Nonprofit Margins (%)

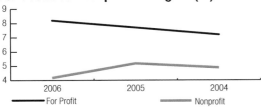

Average Net Premiums Written
($ Billions)

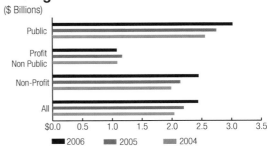

Source: A.M. Best Special Report (8/13/2007)

U.S. Provider-Owned Health Plans

Managed care plans — health maintenance organizations and preferred provider organizations — differ from traditional health insurance in that they restrict health-care provider choices. But they provide a greater range of health benefits for the lowest out-of-pocket expenses.

Historically, provider-owned and affiliated organizations have invested conservatively, and that strategy remained the same in 2006. However, these companies moved away from fixed-income vehicles, placing more of their invested assets in cash and short-term investments.

Distribution of Invested Assets 2006

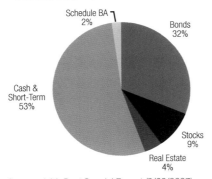

Source: A.M. Best Special Report (9/03/2007)

Lines of Business 2006
(Based on Membership)

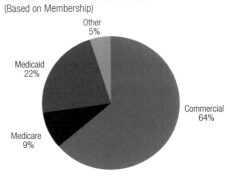

Source: A.M. Best Special Report (9/17/2007)

Web extra: Read the 2007 Special Reports — "U.S. Blue Cross & Blue Shield Plans, Profits, Premiums, Membership Continue to Grow for Blues Plans," "U.S. Provider-Owned Invested Assets," and "U.S. Provider-Owned Underwriting Results" — at *www.ambest.com*.

Reinsurance
Sharing the Risks

WHAT IS REINSURANCE? A way for property/casualty, life and health insurers to spread their risk. An insurer buys insurance — reinsurance — from a reinsurance company to transfer a portion of the risk. How much risk and what conditions trigger the reinsurance are specified in treaties, but generally, the primary carrier retains a fair amount of the risk.

BASIC SCENARIO: An office building is worth $20 million. A primary carrier may be willing to accept the first $10 million in losses, and then cede the rest to a reinsurer. If losses at the building were to exceed the primary layer of $10 million in coverage, say $14 million, then the reinsurer would be called upon to cover the remaining $4 million.

At the Market: Reinsurance

Stock Performance: A six-month look at Reinsurance (AMBGR)
(Six months ended 6/28/2007)
Index, Dec. 31, 2004 = 1000

A.M. Best's Global Reinsurance Index (AMBGR)

| 1,420 – |
| 1,392 – |
| 1,364 – |
| 1,336 – |
| 1,308 – |
| 1,280 – |

Jan Feb   Apr   Jun

Top 10 Global Reinsurance Groups

Ranked by Consolidated Gross Premium Written 2006 ($ Billions)

	Broker	Total Revenues 2006
1	Swiss Re Group	$28.4
2	Munich Re	$27.3
3	Berkshire Hathaway Group	$14.1
4	Hannover Re	$12.3
5	Lloyd's of London	$10.9
6	RGA Reins Co	$4.7
7	Everest Re Group	$4.0
8	Transatlantic Hldgs Inc Group	$4.0
9	SCOR Group	$3.9
10	Partner Re Group	$3.7

Source: 2007 Special Report: "Global Reinsurance - 2006 Market Review. Reinsurers Turn Cautious as Climate Shifts" (8/13/07)

Top 10 Global Reinsurance Brokers

($ Millions)

	Broker	Total Revenues 2006
1	Aon Re Global	$922.0
2	Guy Carpenter & Co. Inc.	$880.0
3	Benfield Group Ltd.	$696.0
4	Willis Re	$597.7
5	Towers Perrin	$165.0 *
6	Cooper Gay (Holdings) Ltd.	$133.2
7	BMS Group	$107.8
8	JLT Reinsurance Brokers Ltd.	$86.4
9	Gallagher Re.	___ **
10	Collins	$59.0

Source: Best's Review (08/2007)
*Reinsurance brokerage revenues only
** Gallagher Re declined to provide 2006 revenue.
This ranking is based on published reports.

Asia: An Evolving Market

EMERGING POWERHOUSE: The Asian reinsurance market is made up of four large markets — Japan, Australia, Korea and China — and two mid-sized markets — Taiwan and India. The remaining countries in the region fall into a small-market category. The nonlife market has been seeing robust growth, leading to an surge in the overall Asian market. Other Asian reinsurance markets that are showing high growth are retakaful and life and casualty reinsurance.

WHAT DOES IT MEAN?

RETAKAFUL: A form of reinsurance for takaful, which is insurance which complies with Islamic law and is a practice whereby individuals in the community jointly guarantee themselves against loss or damage. The word takaful comes from the Arabic language, and it means "guaranteeing each other."

Asian Market: Net Premiums Written[1]

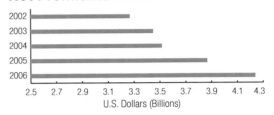

Net Income[1]

Combined Ratio[2]

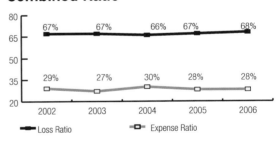

Source: A.M. Best Special Report: Global Reinsurance - 2006 Market Review. Reinsurers Turn Cautious as Climate Shifts (8/13/07)
[1] All AMBAP-rated reinsurers, excluding General Insurance Corporation of India due to unavailability of 2006 data.
[2] All AMBAP-rated reinsurers, excluding Toa Re (as it is exposed to U.S. and European risk) and General Insurance Corporation of India, as it is obliged to write motor business, which has a very high loss ratio.

The Oriental Pearl Tower, Shanghai, China

Bermuda: A Thriving Industry

THE TIDE IS HIGH: Most of the leading property/casualty reinsurers are domiciled in Europe and the United States, but a contingent of reinsurers based in Bermuda are gaining market share. In 2006, the Bermuda market reported a very healthy combined ratio of 83.7, compared to a catastrophic combined ratio of 119.4 for 2005 caused by a chaotic hurricane season.

Bermuda Market: 2004-2006 Key Figure Changes

Low catastrophic losses resulted in extraordinary 2006 for the Bermuda market.
($ Thousands)

	Year End 2005 [1]	Year End 2006 [2]	% Change
Total Equity [1,2]	$47,376,590	$66,970,049	24.30%
Net Premiums Written	42,667,076	43,837,288	2.70%
Losses & LAE	39,013,157	23,635,359	-39.40%
Operating Expenses	11,319,445	11,934,218	5.40%
Net Income	-3,262,603	11,645,772	n.a.
Loss & LAE Ratio	92.80%	55.60%	
Expense Ratio	26.50%	28.10%	
Combined Ratio	119.40%	83.70%	
Return on Equity	-7.00%	19.30%	

(1) - YE 2005 total equity excludes Class of 2005.
(2) - Class of 2005 included in Dec. 31, 2006 total equity and annual change.
Source: A.M. Best Co.

Nonlife Combined Ratios

2006 (GAAP basis)

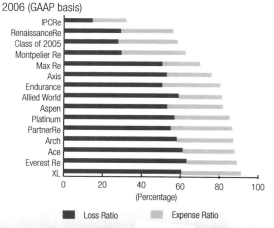

Loss Ratio   Expense Ratio

* Class of 2005 refers to the reinsurance companies established in Bermuda that year in response to catastrophic insured losses sustained as a result of Hurricane Katrina.

Nonlife Net Premium Written

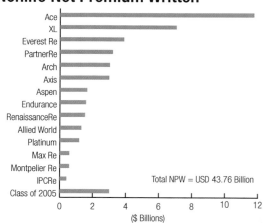

Total NPW = USD 43.76 Billion

Source: A.M. Best Special Report: "Changing Tide of 2006 Storm Activity Showers Benefits on Bermuda's Insurers" (5/28/2007)

Hamilton, Bermuda

Captive Domiciles
Filling in the gaps

WHAT ARE CAPTIVES? A form of self-insurance. Captives are insurers that are created by one or more noninsurance companies to insure their own risks where the conventional insurance market cannot provide coverage or where there is an opportunity for cost reduction.

Single Parent Captive — A captive insurer owned by one company.

Group or Association Captive — A captive owned by two or more companies engaged in similar business to share the collective risks of that industry.

Risk Retention Groups (RRG) — Similar to a group captive, it is a federally created liability insurance company for its members — often trade or professional associations — who share similar risks.

WHERE ARE THEY? Captives are domiciled either in a country outside the United States or in a state that authorizes them.

DID YOU KNOW?

IN THE UNITED STATES, Vermont has the most captives, with 800, followed by Hawaii, with 160, according to the Captive Insurance Companies Association. Outside the United States, Bermuda has the most with 989, followed by the Cayman Islands with 740.

Web extra: For more on captive domiciles, including a complete list, and to read the 2007 Special Report: "U.S. Captive Insurers – Market Review," log onto *www.ambest.com*.

U.S. Domiciled Captives: Net Premiums Written

Although captive insurers posted a fourth straight year of growth in 2006, the pace of net premiums written slowed to a 2.7% increase.

($ Millions)

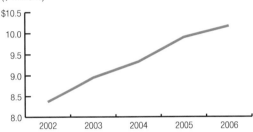

Top Lines

The high cost of medical malpractice insurance continues to push many physicians and other medical professionals away from the traditional market to a captive. The top 5 lines make up nearly three-quarters of the captive market.

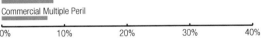

Year-End Surplus

The aggregate growth in surplus in 2006 was 10.3%, an improvement on the pace from 2001 through 2005.

($ Billions)

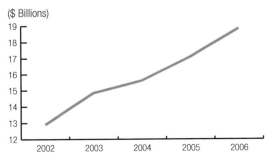

Source: A.M. Best Special Report (7/30/2007)

Regulation: Federal Government
Washington's Watchdogs

Congress creates laws and funding to implement policy through these agencies:

U.S. DEPARTMENT OF THE TREASURY (www.ustreas.gov)

• **Office of the Comptroller of the Currency** (www.occ. treas.gov) Regulates banks' insurance powers

• **Internal Revenue Service** (www.irs.gov) Enforcement authority includes treatment of life and savings products; taxation of mutual vs. stock companies; captive insurers; taxation of brokers' income earned overseas; and offshore insurers.

• **Office of Thrift Supervision** (www.ots.treas.gov) Regulates thrifts established by insurers.

• **Office of Financial Institutions** (www.ustreas.gov/ offices/domestic-finance/financial-institution) Oversees the federal terrorism insurance backstop established by

Congress. Also reviews OCC and OTS regulations for consistency with White House policy.

U.S. DEPARTMENT OF HEALTH AND HUMAN SERVICES (www.hhs.gov)

• **Centers for Medicare & Medicaid Services** (cms.hhs. gov) Oversees Medicare Advantage, the managed-care Medicare program.

U.S. DEPARTMENT OF LABOR (www.dol.gov)

Enforces the Employee Retirement Income Security Act of 1974, which governs many employee-benefit plans, as well as the Health Insurance Portability and Accountability Act, which changed continuation coverage rules under COBRA. Also regulates privacy protection of personal health information.

• **Occupational Safety and Health Administration** (www. osha.gov) Responsible for ergonomics standards, which insurers watch carefully for encroachment on workers' compensation laws.

U.S. DEPARTMENT OF DEFENSE (www.dod.gov)

Runs Tricare health-benefits plan for members of uniformed services, administered regionally by health insurers.

U.S. SECURITIES AND EXCHANGE COMMISSION (www.sec.gov)

Enforces financial reporting under generally accepted accounting principles developed by the Financial Accounting Standards Board. Also helps regulate sales of variable life and annuity products.

U.S. ENVIRONMENTAL PROTECTION AGENCY (www.epa.gov) Oversees Superfund Program.

FEDERAL EMERGENCY MANAGEMENT AGENCY (www.fema.gov) Oversees National Flood Insurance Program.

IN THE BELTWAY
WITH THE McCARRAN-FERGUSON ACT, signed in 1945, Congress granted states a limited exemption from federal anti-trust legislation, declaring that states would continue to regulate the insurance business. The following House and Senate committees deal with insurance issues.

KEY HOUSE COMMITTEES:
• Financial Services
• Ways and Means
• Education and Labor
• Energy and Commerce
• Appropriations

KEY SENATE COMMITTEES:
• Banking, Housing and Urban Affairs
• Finance
• Judiciary
• Health, Education, Labor and Pensions
• Commerce, Science and Transportation
• Agriculture, Nutrition and Forestry
• Small Business & Entrepreneurship

Nongovernmental organizations
Power Sources

Nongovernmental organizations wield de facto authority, often channeled through government agencies.

FINANCIAL INDUSTRY REGULATORY AUTHORITY
(www.finra.org)

Formerly the National Association of Securities Dealers (NASD), FINRA, created in July 2007, is the largest nongovernmental regulator for all securities firms doing business in the United States, overseeing nearly 5,100 brokerage firms, about 173,000 branch offices and more than 669,000 registered securities representatives.

FINANCIAL ACCOUNTING STANDARDS BOARD
(www.fasb.org)

Maintains generally accepted accounting principles used by publicly traded companies. Generally, filings with the SEC conform to GAAP (Generally Accepted Accounting Principles).

INSURANCE SERVICES OFFICE INC. (www.iso.com)

Develops standard forms for many property/casualty lines; files them with state regulators for insurers to use in lieu of developing their own policy forms.

NATIONAL COUNCIL ON COMPENSATION INSURANCE
(www.ncci.com)

Files advisory loss costs for workers' compensation in nearly 40 states, using data developed through reports by members.

INSURANCE MARKETPLACE STANDARDS ASSOCIATION
(www.imsaethics.org)

Promotes ethical conduct in sales and service by member companies, which write life and long-term-care insurance and annuities.

RATING AGENCIES

Rates the financial strength and commercial debt of insurance companies, thereby influencing their financial management, their cost of capital, and their position in the wholesale and retail insurance markets.

DID YOU KNOW?
THE INTERNATIONAL ASSOCIATION OF INSURANCE SUPERVISORS (www.iaisweb.org), based in Basel, Switzerland, was formed in 1994 to protect consumers from unscrupulous business entities. The IAIS, which represents insurance supervisory authorities in some 100 jurisdictions, promotes cooperation among regulators, sets supervision standards, provides member training, and coordinates work with regulators in other financial sectors.

Basel, Switzerland

Who's in charge:
A state-by-state look

Alabama: Walter A. Bell, Insurance Commissioner, 201 Monroe St., Suite 1700, Montgomery, AL 36104, (334) 269-3550, www.aldoi.gov

Alaska: Linda Hall, Director of Insurance, 550 West 7th Ave., Suite 1560, Anchorage, AK 99501-3567, (907) 269-7900, www.dced.state.ak.us/insurance

American Samoa: Laloulu Tagoilelagi, Insurance Commissioner, American Samoa Government, Executive Office Building, Pago Pago, American Samoa 96799, 011-684-633-4116, ext. 240, www.samoanet.com/asg

Arizona: Christina Urias, Director of Insurance, 2910 North 44th St., Suite 210, Phoenix, AZ 85018-7256, (602) 364-3100, www.id.state.az.us

Arkansas: Julie Benafield Bowman, Insurance Commissioner, 1200 West 3rd St., Little Rock, AR 72201-1904, (501) 371-2600, http://insurance.arkansas.gov

California: Steve Poizner, Insurance Commissioner, 300 Capitol Mall, Suite 1700, Sacramento, CA 95814, (916) 492-3500, www.insurance.ca.gov

Colorado: Marcy Morrison, Insurance Commissioner, 1560 Broadway, Suite 850 , Denver, CO 80202, (303) 894-7425, www.dora.state.co.us/insurance

Connecticut: Thomas R. Sullivan, Insurance Commissioner, P.O. Box 816, Hartford, CT 06142-0816, (860) 297-3800, www.ct.gov/cid

Delaware: Matthew Denn, Insurance Commissioner, Rodney Building, 841 Silver Lake Blvd., Dover, DE 19904, (302) 674-7300, www.delawareinsurance.gov

Washington D.C.: Thomas E. Hampton, Insurance Commissioner, 810 First St. NE, Suite 701, Washington, DC 20002, (202) 727-8000, www.disr.dc.gov/disr

Florida: Kevin McCarty, Insurance Commissioner, The Larson Building, 200 E. Gaines St., Room 101, Tallahassee, FL 32399-0301, (850) 413-2526, www.floir.com

Georgia: John W. Oxendine, Insurance Commissioner, 2 Martin Luther King Jr. Drive, West Tower, Suite 704, Atlanta, GA 30334, (404) 656-2056, www.gainsurance.org

Guam: Artemio B. Ilagan, Director of Revenue and Taxation, Tower Government of Guam, P.O. Box 23607, GMF, Guam 96921, (671) 475-1843, www.guamtax.com

Hawaii: Jeffrey P. Schmidt, Insurance Commissioner, Department of Commerce and Consumer Affairs, P.O. Box 3614, Honolulu, HI 96813, (808) 586-2790, www.hawaii.gov/dcca/areas/ins

Idaho: William W. Deal, Director of Insurance, 700 West State St., 3rd Floor, Boise, ID 83720-0043, (208) 334-4250, www.doi.idaho.gov

Illinois: Michael T. McRaith, Director of Insurance, 100 W. Randolph, Suite 9-301, Chicago, IL 60601-3251, (217) 785-5516, www.idfpr.com

Indiana: Jim Atterholt, Insurance Commissioner, 311 W. Washington St. Suite 300, Indianapolis, IN 62767-1678, (317) 232-2385, www.in.gov/idoi

Iowa: Susan Voss, Insurance Commissioner, 330 E. Maple St., Des Moines, IA 50319, (515) 281-5705, www.iid.state.ia.us

Kansas: Sandy Praeger, Insurance Commissioner, 420 SW 9th St., Topeka, KS 66612-1678, (785) 296-3071, www.ksinsurance.org

Kentucky: Julie Mix McPeak, Executive Director, P. O. Box 517, Frankfort, KY 40602-0517, (502) 564-6027/3630, http://doi.ppr.ky.gov

Louisiana: James Donelon, Insurance Commissioner, P.O Box 94214, Baton Rouge, LA 70802, (225) 342-5423, www.ldi.state.la.us

Maine: Eric Cioppa, Acting Superintendent of Insurance, State Office Building Station 34, Augusta, ME 04333-0034, (207) 624-8475, www.maineinsurancereg.org

Maryland: Peggy J. Watson, Interim Insurance Commissioner, 525 St. Paul Place, Baltimore, MD 21202-2272, (410) 468-2090, www.mdinsurance.state.md.us

Massachusetts: Nonnie S. Burnes, Commissioner of Insurance, 1 South Station, 5th Floor, Boston, MA 02210, (617) 521-7301, www.mass.gov/doi

Michigan: Linda A. Watters, Insurance Commissioner, Office of Financial and Insurance Services Ottawa Building, 3rd Floor 611 W. Ottawa, Lansing, MI 48933-1070, (517) 373-0220, www.michigan.gov/ofis

Minnesota: Glenn Wilson, Insurance Commissioner, 85 7th Place East Suite 500, St. Paul, MN 55101-2198, (651) 296-6025, www.commerce.state.mn.us

Mississippi: George Dale, Director of Insurance, 1001 Wollfork St. Building 501 N. West St., Jackson, MS 39201, (601) 359-3569, www.doi.state.ms.us

Missouri: Douglas Ommen, Director of Insurance, 301 W. High St. Suite 530, Jefferson City, MO 65102, (573) 751-4126, www.insurance.mo.gov

Montana: John Morrison, Montana State Auditor, the Commissioner of Insurance and Securities, 840 Helena Ave. , Helena, MT 59601, (406) 444-2040, www.sao.mt.gov

Nebraska: Ann Frohman, Acting Director of Insurance, 941 O St., Suite 400, Lincoln, NE 68508, (402) 471-2201, www.doi.ne.gov

Nevada: Alice A. Molasky-Arman, Insurance Commissioner, 788 Fairview Drive, Suite 300, Carson City, NV 89701, (775) 687-4270, www.doi.state.nv.us

New Hampshire: Roger A. Sevigny, Insurance Commissioner, 21 South Fruit St., Suite 14, Concord, NH 03301, (603) 271-2261, www.nh.gov/insurance

New Jersey: Steven Goldman, Insurance Commissioner, P.O. Box 325, Trenton, NJ 08625-0325, (609) 292-5360, www.njdobi.org

New Mexico: Morris Chavez, Superintendent of Insurance, P.O. Drawer 1269, Santa Fe, NM 87504-1269, (505) 827-4601, http://www.nmprc.state.nm.us/id.htm

New York: Eric Dinallo, Superintendent of Insurance, 25 Beaver Street, New York, NY 10004-2319, (212) 480-2289, www.ins.state.ny.us

North Carolina: Jim Long, Insurance Commissioner, 1201 Mail Service Center, Raleigh, NC 27699-1201, (919) 733-3058, www.ncdoi.com

North Dakota: Adam Hamm, Insurance Commissioner, 600 E. Boulevard, Bismarck, ND 58505-0320, (701) 328-2440, www.state.nd.us/ndins

Ohio: Mary Jo Hudson, Director of Insurance, 2100 Stella Court, Columbus, OH 43215-1067, (614) 644-2658, www.ohioinsurance.gov

 Oklahoma: Kim Holland, Insurance Commissioner, 2401 NW 23rd St., Suite 28, Oklahoma City, OK 73107, (405) 522-2828, www.oid.state.ok.us

 Oregon: Carl Lundberg, Interim Insurance Administrator, P.O. 14480, Salem, OR 97309-0405, (503) 947-7202, www.insurance.oregon.gov

 Pennsylvania: Joel Ario, Acting Insurance Commissioner, 1326 Strawberry Square, Harrisburg, PA 17120, (717) 783-0442, http://www.ins.state.pa.us

 Puerto Rico: Dorelisse Juarbe Jimenez, Insurance Commissioner, 1607 Ponce de Leon Ave. , Santurce, Puerto Rico 00909, (787) 722-8686, http://www.gobierno.pr

 Rhode Island: Joseph Torti III, Superintendent of Insurance, 233 Richmond St., Suite 233, Providence, RI 02903-4233, (401) 222-2223, www.dbr.state.ri.us

 South Carolina: Scott H. Richardson, Director of Insurance, 300 Arbor Lake Drive, Suite 1200, Columbia, SC 29223, (803) 737-6212, www.doi.sc.gov

 South Dakota: Merle D. Scheiber, Director of Insurance, 445 East Capitol Ave., Pierre, SD 57501, (605) 773-3563, www.state.sd.us/drr2/reg/insurance/

 Tennessee: Leslie A. Newman, Insurance Commissioner, Davy Crockett Tower, Fifth Floor, 500 James Robertson Parkway, Nashville, TN 37243-0565, (615) 741-6007, www.state.tn.us/commerce/insurance/index.html

 Texas: Mike Geeslin, Insurance Commissioner, P.O. Box 149104, Austin, TX 78701, (512) 463-6464, www.tdi.state.tx.us

 Utah: Kent Michie, Insurance Commissioner, 3110 State Office Building, Salt Lake City, UT 84114-1201, (801) 538-3800, www.insurance.utah.gov

 Vermont: Paulette Thabault, Commissioner of Banking, Insurance, Securities and Health Care Administration, 89 Main St., Drawer 20, Montpelier, VT 05620-3101, (802) 828-3301, www.bishca.state.vt.us

 Virginia: Alfred W. Gross, Insurance Commissioner, P.O. Box 1157, Richmond, VA 23218, (804) 371-9741, www.scc.virginia.gov/division/boi/index.htm

 Virgin Islands: Gregory Francis, Lieutenant Governor/Insurance Commissioner, 18 Kongens Gade, Charlotte Amalie, St. Thomas 00802, (340) 774-2991, http://www.governordejongh.com

 Washington: Mike Bradley Kreidler, Insurance Commissioner, P.O. Box 40255, Olympia, WA 98504-0255, (360) 725-7100, http://www.insurance.wa.gov

 West Virginia: Jane L. Cline, Insurance Commissioner, P.O. Box 50540, Charleston, WV 25305-0540, (304) 558-3354, www.wvinsurance.gov

 Wisconsin: Sean Dilweg, Insurance Commissioner, P.O. Box 7873, Madison, WI 53707-7873, (608) 267-1233, www.oci.wi.gov

 Wyoming: Ken Vines, Insurance Commissioner, 122 W. 25th St., 3rd East, Cheyenne, WY 82002-0440, (307) 777-7401, http://insurance.state.wy.us

---

DID YOU KNOW?

IN 2006, STATES PAID a total of $15.4 billion in premium taxes, based on the volume of insurance written. Leading the way was California, with $2.2 billion, followed by Texas, which paid $1.2 billion, according to the U.S. Census Bureau.

Who's in charge:

A province-by-province look

Office of the Superintendent of Financial Institutions: Julie Dickson, Acting Superintendent of Financial Institutions, 255 Albert St., Ottawa, Canada K1A 0H2, (613) 990-3667, www.osfi-bsif.gc.ca

Alberta: Arthur Hagan, Deputy Superintendent, Regulation and Market Conduct, 402 Terrace Building 9515-107 St., Edmonton, Alberta AB T5K 2C3, (780) 415-9226, www.finance.gov.ab.ca/business/insurance

British Columbia: Michael Grist, Deputy Superintendent, Insurance and Pensions, Suite 1200, 13450 102nd Ave., Surrey, British Columbia V3T 5X3, (604) 953-5370, www.fic.gov.bc.ca

Manitoba: Jim Scalena, Superintendent of Financial Institutions, 1115-405 Broadway Ave., Winnipeg, Manitoba R3C 3L6, (204) 945-2542, www.gov.mb.ca/finance/cca/firb

New Brunswick: Roderick MacKenzie, Superintendent of Insurance,King Tower, 440 King St., Suite 635, Fredericton, New Brunswick E3B 5H8, (506) 453-2512, www.gnb.ca/0062

Newfoundland: Winston Morris, Superintendent of Insurance, Confederation Building, 2nd Floor, West Block P.O. Box 8700, St. John's, Newfoundland and Labrador, A1B 4J6, (709) 729-2570, www.gov.nl.ca

Northwest Territories/Nunavut: Douglas Doak, Superintendent of Insurance 3rd Floor, YK Centre Building, 4822 48th St., Yellowknife, Northwest Territories X1A 1N2, (867) 920-3423, www.gov.nt.ca

Nova Scotia: Doug Murphy, Superintendent of Insurance, Credit Unions and Trust and Loan Companies, 5151 Terminal Road, 7th Floor, Halifax, Nova Scotia B3J 3C8, (902) 424-6331, www.gov.ns.ca

Ontario: Bob Christie, Chief Executive Officer and Superintendent of Financial Services, 5160 Yonge St., 17th Floor, Box 85, Toronto, Ontario M2N 6L9, (416) 590-7000, www.fsco.gov.on.ca

Prince Edward Island: Robert Bradley, Superintendent of Insurance, 105 Rochford St., P.O. Box 2000, Charlottetown, Prince Edward Island C1A 7N8, (902) 368-6478, www.gov.pe.ca/oag/ccaid-info

Quebec: Nancy Chamberland, Executive Director, 2640 Boulevard Laurier, bureau 400, Quebec, G1V 5C1, (877) 525-0337, www.lautorite.qc.ca

Saskatchewan: Jim Hall, Superintendent of Insurance, Suite 601, 1919 Saskatchewan Drive, Regina , Saskatchewan S4P 4H2, (306) 787-7881, http://www.sfsc.gov.sk.ca/financial

Yukon Territory: Fiona Charbonneau, Superintendent of Insurance, P.O. Box 2703 (C-5), Whitehorse, Yukon Territory Y1A 2C6, (867) 667-5111, www.gov.yk.ca

DID YOU KNOW?
IN CANADA, regulation of the property/casualty and life and health insurance companies is shared between the federal government, through the Office of the Superintendent of Financial Institutions, and the provincial governments.

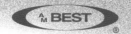

Test Your Knowledge

Across

1. Security against insured loss
4. Its purpose is to ascertain accuracy
6. Home to most captives in U.S.
8. Not net, but _____ premiums
9. Where it's not called nonlife (abbr.)
11. New professional designation (abbr.)
12. London coffee house circa 1688
16. An employee benefit plan, or a restaurant where you serve yourself
18. Fund that absorbs losses
19. A specific type of conversion to a stock insurance company
22. Make a _____
24. A recognized actuary (abbr.)
26. "Red ink" amount
27. Insurance for insurers
31. Negligence of a professional duty that leads to injury
35. A conclusive resolution
38. Type of insurance that protects against loss resulting from death
39. Designated by policyholder
41. Insurance seller
42. Transit over land
43. Most threatened by a tornado, according to modelers (abbr.)
44. Opposite of loss
47. Not bankrupt, but _____
49. Opinion of ability to pay claims
52. Type of policy in effect for the life of the insured
53. What insured pays in a claim

Down

2. Where an insurance company is incorporated
3. A reinsurance giant, founded in 1880: _____ Re
4. Unexpected, unforeseen event
5. Covered
7. Sum total
10. Time between a transaction and funds are drawn to cover it
13. Where most Canadians live
14. What an insurer needs to do business
15. Great loss, misfortune
17. Type of life insurance; in effect for a limited period
20. Carcinogen that has cost insurers billions
21. Often, how the size of a life/health insurance company is measured (2 words)
22. Where Northridge Earthquake occurred
23. All of the property owned by a carrier
25. A stock indicator of insurance industry companies
28. Who regulates insurance
29. Managed care groups
30. Devastating 2005 hurricane
32. The insurance industry's mathematician
33. Pays a periodic income benefit
34. 2005's other monster storm
36. Risk
37. _____ bonds protect against acts of employee dishonesty
39. Forms of suretyship
40. Something lost or surrendered as a penalty
43. Bottom line
44. Medicare segment that covers cost of prescription drugs
45. Not inland, but _____
46. _____ lines are associated with fire insurance
48. Peril not covered by fed flood program ... yet
50. Act of _____
51. Makes it possible to buy a home with a 5% down payment (abbr.)

See page 60 for answers.

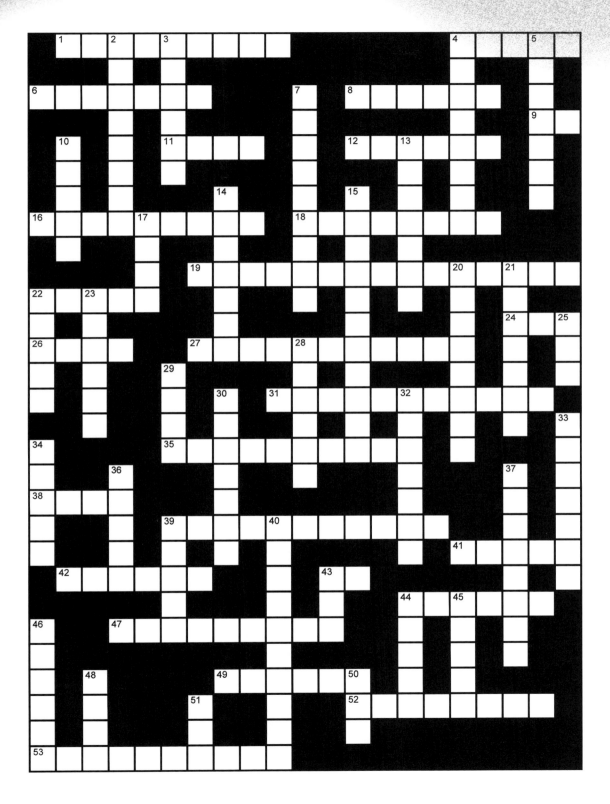

Find the insurance-related word

1. actuary
2. broker
3. captive
4. casualty
5. compulsory
6. coverage
7. domicile
8. equity

9. exposure
10. fellow
11. group
12. hazard
13. health
14. impairment
15. lapse
16. liability

17. liquidity
18. mature
19. medicare
20. mutual
21. obligee
22. property
23. ratio
24. sidecar

25. solvency
26. stock
27. surety
28. surplus
29. term
30. valuation

See page 60 for answers.

```
H S U R E T Y T Y X W X E N C S F T Q V
A E G R O U P R R W F L D R U F I Q A R
Z W A N S J A E B G I M P A I R M E N T
A R T L O U K L E C O M P U L S O R Y F
R I V C T O W R I J R I B M J Y T F T F
D U P C R H U M W Q C A S U A L T Y L F
J S A B L S O O G R U U J R Z T A A N K
W O T V O D L R L K B I A R Z J U T F E
D L U P M L J A I Q Z C D X I T M R K R
V V X N E D Y T A B E B O I U D V W E G
C E D F L T O I B D W G S M T L A P S E
A N I Y I E B O I U I K F U O Y D J M I
P C H U L P L S L Y C O V E R A G E W Y
T Y Q F C W I X I O Z P P R O P E R T Y
I E P Z O A G M T V V L B F K V L G N Y
V X R O B W E S Y M E D I C A R E U F B
E N D M M T E K V A L U A T I O N U S I
```

NEED AN EXPERT?

Insurance professionals and aspiring professionals have opportunities to increase their knowledge of the industry through classes leading to an insurance designation that recognizes expertise.

Insurance Professional Designations

Accredited Adviser in Insurance (AAI)

Accredited Asset Management Specialist (AAMS)

Accredited Estate Planner (AEP)

Accredited Financial Counselor (AFC)

Accredited Pension Administrator (APA)

Accredited Pension Representative (APR)

Associate Financial Advisor (AFA)

Associate in Claims (AIC)

Associate in Commercial Underwriting (AU)

Associate in Fidelity and Surety Bonding (AFSB)

Associate in Information Technology (AIT)

Associate in Insurance Accounting and Finance (AIAF)

Associate in Insurance Accounting & Finance
   (Life/Health Track) (AIAF)

Associate in Insurance Services (AIS)

Associate in Management (AIM)

Associate in Marine Insurance Management (AMIM)

Associate in Personal Insurance (API)

Associate in Premium Auditing (APA)

Associate in Regulation and Compliance (ARC)

Associate in Reinsurance (ARe)

Associate in Risk Management (ARM)

Associate in Risk Management for Public Entities (ARM-P)

Associate in Surplus Lines Insurance (ASLI)

Associate of the Casualty Actuarial Society (ACAS)

Associate of the Conference of Consulting Actuaries (ACA)

Associate, Annuity Products & Administration (AAPA)

Associate, Customer Service Program (ACS)

Associate, Financial Services Institute (AFSI)

Associate, Insurance Agency Administration (AIAA)

Associate, Insurance Regulatory Compliance (AIRC)

Associate, Life Management Institute (ALMI)

Associate, Reinsurance Administration (ARA)

Associate, Society of Actuaries (ASA)

Automobile Claim Law Associate (ACLA)

Automobile Claim Law Specialist (ACLS)

Board Certified in Estate Planning (BCE)

60 YEARS LATER, A NEW CREDENTIAL

To aid businesses that are increasingly seeking out risk analysts, managers and chief risk officers, the Society of Actuaries has issued its first new credential since its founding nearly 60 years ago.

Called the Chartered Enterprise Risk Analyst credential (CERA), the designation can be earned by professionals who successfully complete the curriculum that includes the most comprehensive demonstration of enterprise risk management available.

The new designation is the SOA's first since its founding in 1949, when the Fellow of the Society of Actuaries (FSA) and Associate of the Society of Actuaries (ASA) credentials were established.

The new designation by the SOA, the largest professional, actuarial organization in the world, is the result of its research that shows that actuarial credentials are very highly regarded among employers in insurance, reinsurance and consulting markets.

Topics reviewed within the curriculum include:
- probability
- financial mathematics
- financial economics
- micro and macro economics
- construction of actuarial models
- advanced finance and enterprise risk management
- financial reporting and operational risk
- professionalism

Professionals, on average, will spend three to four years to obtain a CERA credential. Actuaries spend a lot of time dealing with numbers in order to estimate risks and returns. In doing so, they enable smart and more confident financial planning decisions.

Actuaries spend a lot of time dealing with numbers in order to estimate risks and returns. In doing so, they enable smart and more confident financial planning decisions.

NEED AN EXPERT? (continued)

Casualty Claim Law Associate (CCLA)
Casualty Claim Law Specialist (CCLS)
Certified Annuity Advisor (CAA)
Certified Annuity Specialist (CAS)
Certified Employee Benefit Specialist (CEBS)
Certified Estate Advisor (CEA)
Certified Estate Planner (CEP)
Certified Financial Planner (CFP)
Certified Fund Specialist (CFS)
Certified in Long-Term Care (CLTC)
Certified Insurance Counselor (CIC)
Certified Insurance Service Representative (CISR)
Certified Investment Management Analyst (CIMA)
Certified Pension Consultant (CPC)
Certified Professional Insurance Woman/Man (CPIW/M)
Certified Risk Managers International (CRM)
Certified Senior Advisor (CSA)
Chartered Advisor for Senior Living (CASL)
Chartered Enterprise Risk Analyst (CERA)
Chartered Financial Analyst (CFA)
Chartered Financial Consultant (ChFC)
Chartered Leadership Fellow (CLF)
Chartered Life Underwriter (CLU)
Chartered Mutual Fund Counselor (CMFC)
Chartered Property Casualty Underwriter (CPCU)
Chartered Retirement Planning Counselor (CRPC)
Chartered Retirement Plans Specialist (CRPS)
Chartered Senior Financial Planner (CSFP)
Disability Healthcare Professional (DHP)
Disability Income Associate (DIA)
Diversified Advanced Education (DAE)
Employee Healthcare Benefits Associate (EHBA)
Fellow of the Casualty Actuarial Society (FCAS)
Fellow of the Conference of Consulting Actuaries (FCA)
Fellow, Financial Services Institute (FFSI)
Fellow, Life Management Institute (FLMI)
Fellow, Society of Actuaries (FSA)
Fellow, Society of Pension Actuaries (FSPA)
Financial Services Specialist (FSS)
Fraud Claim Law Associate (FCLA)
Fraud Claim Law Specialist (FCLS)
Health Care Anti-Fraud Associate (HCAFA)

Health Insurance Associate (HIA)
Healthcare Customer Service Associate (HCSA)
HIPAA Associate (Health Insurance Portability and Accountability Act) (HIPAAA)
HIPAA Professional (Health Insurance Portability and Accountability Act) (HIPAAP)
Insurance Training Professional (ITP)
Legal Principles Claim Specialist (LPCS)
Life Underwriters Training Council Fellow (LUTCF)
Long-Term Care Professional (LTCP)
Managed Healthcare Professional (MHP)
Master Financial Advisor (MFA)
Medical Management Associate (MMA)
Member, American Academy of Actuaries (MAAA)
Member, Society of Pension Actuaries (MSPA)
Private Annuity Trusts Adviser (PATA)
Professional Financial Advisor (PFA)
Professional, Customer Service (PCS)
Property Claim Law Associate (PCLA)
Property Claim Law Specialist (PCLS)
Qualified 401(k) Administrator (QKA)
Qualified Pension Administrator (QPA)
Qualified Plan Financial Consultant (QPFC)
Registered Employee Benefits Consultant (REBC)
Registered Health Underwriters (RHU)
Registered Professional Liability Underwriter (RPLU)
RIMS Fellow (RF)
Senior Claim Law Associate (SCLA)
Workers' Compensation Claim Law Associate (WCLA)
Workers' Compensation Claim Law Specialist (WCLS)

Web extra: A full description of each designation can be found in the May 2007 issue of *Best's Review* and in the online archive at *www.ambest.com.*

10 Meetings You Don't Want To Miss

Annual conventions for some of the largest trade organizations that cater to the specialties within the worldwide insurance arena. Log onto **www3.ambest.com/review/convsearch/meetsrch.asp** for Best's directory of meetings.

1 American Council of Life Insurers: ACLI 2008 Annual Conference, Boston, October 19-21, 2008 **(www.acli.org)**

2 America's Health Insurance Plans: Institute 2008: AHIP Annual Meeting, San Francisco, June 18-20, 2008. **(www.ahip.org/conferences)**

3 Les Rendez-Vous de Septembre: 2008 International Convention of Insurers, Reinsurers, Brokers and Reinsurance Consultants, Monte Carlo, Monaco, September 6-12, 2008 **(www.rvs-monte-carlo.com)**

4 National Association of Health Underwriters: 2008 Annual Convention & Exhibition, San Diego, June 29-July 2, 2008 **(www.nahu.org)**

5 National Association of Mutual Insurance Companies: 2008 Annual Convention, Philadelphia, September 28-October 1, 2008 **(www.namic.org)**

6 National Association of Professional Surplus Lines Offices: 2008 Annual Convention, San Diego, September 10-13, 2008 **(www.napslo.org)**

7 Property Casualty Insurers Association of America: 2008 PCI Annual Meeting, Scottsdale, Ariz., October 27-30, 2008 **(www.pciaa.net)**

8 Risk Insurance and Management Society, Inc.: RIMS 2008 Annual Conference & Exhibition, San Diego, April 27-May 1, 2008 **(www.rims.org)**

9 Risk Insurance and Management Society, Inc. in Canada: RIMS Canada 2008 Annual Conference, Toronto, September 21-24, 2008 **(http://rimscanada.rims.org)**

10 Vermont Captive Insurance Association: 2008 Annual Conference, Burlington, Vt., August 12-14, 2008 **(www.vcia.com)**

Puzzle Answers

Answers to Word Search on page 56.

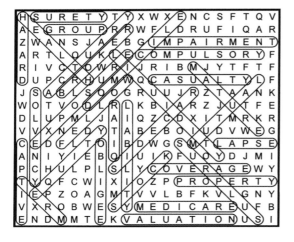

Answers to crossword puzzle on page 54-55.

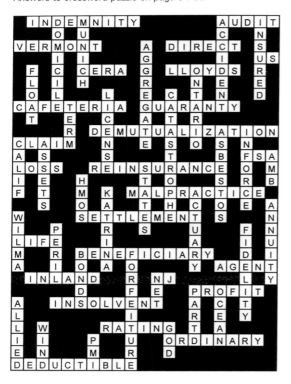

Answers to Athletes/Celebrities puzzle on page 2-3.

1. Michael Flatley

2. Mark McGwire

3. America Ferrera, star of "Ugly Betty"

4. Secretariat

5. Bruce Springsteen

6. Claudia Schiffer

7. Keith Richards

8. Betty Grable

9. Bette Davis

10. Charlie Chaplin

11. Jimmy Durante

2047283